MW00855666

Living Hope

Paul W. Chilcote
and Steve Harper

LIVING
HOPE

*AN INCLUSIVE VISION
OF THE FUTURE*

CASCADE *Books* • Eugene, Oregon

LIVING HOPE
An Inclusive Vision of the Future

Copyright © 2020 Paul W. Chilcote and Steve Harper. All rights reserved.
Except for brief quotations in critical publications or reviews, no part of
this book may be reproduced in any manner without prior written permission from the publisher. Write: Permissions, Wipf and Stock Publishers,
199 W. 8th Ave., Suite 3, Eugene, OR 97401.

Cascade Books
An Imprint of Wipf and Stock Publishers
199 W. 8th Ave., Suite 3
Eugene, OR 97401

www.wipfandstock.com

PAPERBACK ISBN: 978-1-7252-7089-3
HARDCOVER ISBN: 978-1-7252-7090-9
EBOOK ISBN: 978-1-7252-7091-6

Cataloguing-in-Publication data:

Names: Chilcote, Paul Wesley, 1954–, author. | Harper, Steve, author.
Title: Living hope : an inclusive vision of the future / Paul W. Chilcote and
    Steve Harper.
Description: Eugene, OR : Cascade Books, 2020 | Includes bibliographical
    references.
Identifiers: ISBN 978-1-7252-7089-3 (paperback) | ISBN 978-1-7252-7090-9
    (hardcover) | ISBN 978-1-7252-7091-6 (ebook)
Subjects: LCSH: Christian life. | Methodist Church—Doctrines. | Hope—
    Religious aspects—Christianity.
Classification: BX8331.2 .C45 2020 (print) | BX8331.2 .C45 (ebook)

Manufactured in the U.S.A.   MAY 7, 2020

To our partners in life,
Janet and Jeannie,
who inspire hope in us every day

CONTENTS

AN UNFETTERED HOPE

"Everyone really struggled," Carolyne explained. "We struggled to deal with the loss of loved ones. We struggled with the inability to live without fear. We struggled to find hope in the hardship." This is how a young Kenyan woman described her life until ZOE Empowers began to help her community name and dismantle the chains that bound them and stole their dreams.[1] Only then were they able to experience the joy, beauty, and power of living hope. This true story of genuine liberation comes from Africa, but it could just as easily come from next door. We all long for an unfettered hope.

Our books *Holy Love* and *Active Faith* appeared in fairly quick succession in 2019. Steve's book on love argued for an inclusive church and a unity-in-diversity based on a biblical theology of human sexuality. Paul's book on faith pressed that argument forward, but also consisted of a progressive Wesleyan declaration rooted in the practices of truth, joy, peace, and love. In both these books we sought to speak into the life of the church in general, but also The United Methodist Church, in particular. Our common hope has been for the church to

---

1. For the full story, see "Orphaned Children Reunite in the Name of Peace."

rediscover what faithfulness and unity mean for a time such as this.

In the conversations we shared around these two publications, an insight dawned upon us rather simultaneously. We have love and we have faith. What about hope? It immediately struck us that what the church and individual followers of Jesus need now, perhaps more than ever, is a heavy dose of hope. These theological virtues—faith, hope, and love—really define our lives as Christians. A trilogy emerged in our minds, and the idea for *Living Hope* was born. On this book, however, unlike the other two, we really wanted to work together.

Readers who are dyed-in-the-wool Methodists might immediately recognize the method here. Chapter 1 provides a panoramic vision of hope in the scriptural witness. The second chapter explores narratives of hope that come out of our Judeo-Christian heritage. Chapter 3 affords a reasoned account for the hope that is in us. And the final chapter seeks to offer ways in which you can experience hope through practices. We find this quadrilateral approach to be helpful: scripture, tradition, reason, and experience.

Both of us are, by nature, hopeful people. We are optimists who prefer to see the glass half full. But we have experienced hopelessness and despair. We need this book as much as you do. All of us need hope right now, like Carolyne and her community in Kenya did. In an era of such deep polarization and rancor, potential division and challenge, we long for authenticity. We yearn for God to show us how we can live into a future filled with hope as God's beloved children. We long for a living hope based on God's inclusive vision of the future.

ONE
THE WITNESS TO HOPE

The witness to hope is rooted in Scripture. The biblical vision of hope begins with creation. In creation God enacts a living hope—a hope that something is coming into existence that will enrich and expand current reality. James Weldon Johnson captured the motivation of this first great act of grace in the opening lines of his poem "The Creation."

> And God stepped out on space,
> And he looked around and said:
> *I'm lonely—*
> *I'll make me a world.*[1]

In a way that defies description, even for God, creation was an act of hope—a hope born of God's desire for relationships in a cosmos filled with wondrous detail that we are still discovering and exploring. Hope arises from the very nature of God, as the Trinity sings and dances everything into being.

---

1. Johnson, *God's Trombones*, 23. "God's Creation" is the first poem, said to have been written in 1919.

Hope in the Old Testament

The Bible adds its own poetry to this picture of living hope through two creation stories. The first story (Gen 1:1—2:4) portrays God's hope with respect to the entire created order, summarizing it in the word *good*—what theologians call original righteousness. Seven times in the first creation story we read that "it was good." God's original vision was for the entire creation to be good in every way. That is, God created everyone and everything to fit into and contribute to a cosmic and eternal goodness.

The second creation story (Gen 2:5–24) continues the same hope for goodness, but focuses it on humanity. God makes Adam and Eve in God's own image. As such, they are incarnations of hope, both in their relationship with each other and as the stewards of hope in their calling to care for the rest of creation. Even after their fall in Genesis 3, God still views human beings as the bearers of hope in the world (Gen 4–11). Moreover, God calls a particular family within the human community, later called the Jews, to be a living illustration of hope (from Gen 12 to the end of the Hebrew Scriptures). God knew that a concrete embodiment of hope was required.

One of the overarching words in the Old Testament for this living hope is *shalom*. Often simply translated "peace," it means much more than this. It points to the establishment of comprehensive wellness and wholeness, beginning with individuals and extending outward to the entire cosmos.[2] It includes the

---

2. Mounce, *Dictionary*, 502–4. The Greek word for peace is *eirene*. The description of peace in this chapter combines the two words because their meanings are similar.

absence of war, but it is not something passive. Shalom refers to the way in which God works to restore and renew all of life; God restores you, me, and the entire cosmos so that God's original intentions can be realized. This includes God's call for us to be peacemakers (Matt 5:9), what today we might refer to as nonviolent resistance. How desperately we need peacemaking today in relation to so many critical concerns and pressing needs. The Bible offers a vision of living hope rooted in the establishment and maintenance of right relationships—completeness, unity, and harmony between everyone and everything. Such hope is God-made and God-given. It is a gift that God offers to us freely out of love, but God also asks us to give it away. As St. Francis put it, we become instruments of God's peace. With respect to hope, we are co-creators with God. As St. Augustine preached: "Without God, we cannot; without us, God will not."[3] Living hope is active love.

The first two chapters of Genesis establish an essential theology of hope. They reveal what creation was meant to be, so that after the fall, we still have a point of reference to reclaim, renew, and restore life as God intends. Hope is not abstract; it is in relation to revelation—a promise-filled revelation.[4] Shalom is not an intangible concept; it is a life to be lived by the grace of God. In the Old Testament we see examples of it. The big Bible word for it is *holiness*—of heart and life. We have a living hope at work within us and through us. We live by hope. We move forward with hope. The Bible says that hope ignites our desire for God. It moves us to seek to "be holy as God is holy"

3. Augustine, "Sermon 169," in *Sermons*, 230.

4. Henri Nouwen connects hope and promise in "'The Promise of Hope," an episode of the *Now & Then* podcast.

(Lev 19:2). The essence of this holiness is love, fulfilled when we respond to the love of God for us by loving God "with all your heart, all your being, and all your strength" (Deut 6:5). Do you see how hope is bound up together with goodness, peace, and love?

Hope inspires us to work for the common good.[5] It has a collective as well as an individual sense. This is the love described in the second great commandment—"love your neighbor as yourself" (Lev 19:18). Micah summed up the essence of external holiness in three phrases: "to do justice, embrace faithful love, and walk humbly with your God" (Mic 6:8). To do justice means that we seek equity, fairness, and inclusion for all. Embracing faithful love means that God's *hesed* (steadfast love) is present and active in and through us.[6] And walking humbly means living in ways that enable us to be instruments of God's peace. In the next chapter we will show how a devotion to the common good has fueled hope in history.

All this is scripted for us in the word *covenant*, a concept that unites the Old and New Testaments. In the Old Testament the Law reveals this relational bond. But law, in this sense, does not mean "rules and regulations." It refers to enacted love— the establishment and maintenance of relationships that are life-giving. Even when sin corrupted the goodness of Eden, covenant love remained a possibility. In the shadow of human brokenness, the Law became a source of hope because a promise

5. Walter Brueggemann develops this in his book *Journey to the Common Good*.

6. Brueggemann describes *hesed* as God's manifestation of compassion, mercy, grace, faithfulness, and forgiveness. He develops each of these attributes in his book, *Theology of the Old Testament*, 215–20. He sees these qualities of God expressed in the name Yahweh.

accompanied the demands of God's commandments—"by doing them one will live" (Lev 18:5). John Wesley modeled his General Rules on this vision of law-plus-promise and the hope it entailed. He never intended his threefold admonition to do no harm, to do good, and to "attend upon the ordinances of God" (meaning to engage in time-honored spiritual practices) as something legal; rather, it was a way of life that promised hope and joy.[7] Through these practices we manifest hope, modeling God's way to others and for the sake of the world. We exhibit holiness of heart and life.

The Old Testament further reveals that living with hope necessarily includes prophetic action. Walter Brueggemann describes this aspect of hope as "interrupting silence."[8] This practice begins when we break our silence about things that need to be addressed through both words and deeds. It continues, Brueggemann maintains, when we refuse to stop speaking and acting despite the efforts of our opponents to silence us. God calls us to speak truth to power whenever, wherever, and however this might be required. We see this hope-creating work in the lives and ministry of Old Testament heroes like Moses and Esther who did this very thing. Through their witness we are reminded that living with hope includes our acceptance of struggle. The journey to the promised land inevitably takes us through some kind of wilderness. Fallen-world imperialism does not take kindly to resistance.

7. Wesley, "The General Rules of the United Societies (1743)," in *Methodist Societies*, 70–73. Rueben Job has written an excellent interpretation of these practices in his book *Three Simple Rules*.

8. Brueggemann, *Interrupting Silence*.

The Old Testament also reveals that a living hope requires us to offer a "light to the nations" and covenant love to others (Isa 42:6). You might call this the missional dimension of living hope. We never really experience the fullness of hope until we participate in God's work to "let justice roll down like waters, and righteousness like an ever-flowing stream" throughout the earth (Amos 5:24). Martin Luther King Jr. simply called this being a good neighbor.[9] Interestingly, along these same lines, Walter Brueggemann sums up the Old Testament's vision of covenant love in the word "neighborliness."[10] Sadly, Israel failed to exhibit this kind of hope. Instead, God's chosen people exchanged their election to service for election to privilege. Instead of being a beacon of hope for others, they hung onto their chosenness in order to feel secure themselves. And this is the perennial danger of those who believe themselves to be close to God. But their failure, and the failure of so many others in the community of faith, does not eclipse the revelation of God's will for our hope to be comprehensive and pervasive.

Jesus Christ: Hope Incarnate

We could say more about living hope as the vision that plays out in the Old Testament. But Jesus, the Word made flesh (John 1:14), actually incarnated God's original vision of hope. We see it more clearly in him than anywhere else. The Common English Bible's designation of Jesus as "The Human One" reminds us that hope can never be separated from real life here and

9. King, *Strength to Love*, 20–29.
10. Brueggemann, *God, Neighbor, Empire*.

now.[11] Hope sprang to life in Jesus' humanity. We see it when he launched his ministry in Nazareth, using Isaiah's words to say that God had sent him to "preach good news to the poor, to proclaim release to the captives, and recovery of sight to the blind, to liberate the oppressed, and to proclaim the year of the Lord's favor" (Luke 4:18–19). Each aspect of his ministry gave hope to others.

Jesus also gave people hope by what he did not say on that occasion. He left out the final phrase of the Isaiah passage (62:2b), which was about exacting God's day of vindication. He omitted that, saying in effect that his ministry would be one of restoration, not retribution. That was a message of hope, especially for those who had heaps of guilt laid upon them by religious leaders who made "breaking the law" the unpardonable sin. Jesus launched a ministry that offered hope to everyone, but especially to those who had been made "less-than" and marginalized in society and by religion.

For the next three years, Jesus "traveled around doing good" (Acts 10:38). Notice the connection of the word *good* to his ministry, the very word used to describe life before the fall in Genesis 3—the very word used to describe life as God intends for it to be. Jesus' whole life and work was redemptive and restorative. His life came to its apex at the cross, that place where atonement (at-one-ment) became a reality. No wonder John Wesley retitled *The Imitation of Christ* by Thomas à Kempis *The Christian's Pattern*. The term *Christlikeness* has been the

---

11. "The Human One" is the CEB translation of the phrase "Son of Man"—not only to make the phrase more inclusive, but to clearly show that Jesus' life is a realistic and realizable model for our living. In the New Testament, John's phrase "abiding in Christ" (John 15) refers to abundant living.

one-word summary of the Christian life across the centuries.[12] While Jesus died, he continues to live as the universal Christ whose cosmic existence gives us hope that death is not the last word for us and that all life is headed toward a grand consummation (Eph 1:9–10).

Jesus' Message of Hope

Jesus' departure from this world did not leave us orphaned. He left us with the message and the means for continuing to live in hope and to offer hope to others. He embedded that message of hope particularly in what he taught about the kingdom of God.[13] The kingdom or reign of God functions as a focal point for our own theology of hope because it combines the realities of hope that we see in the present moment (the "already") and the future fulfillment of hope that we are not yet able to see (the "not yet"). We become co-creators with God in the movement from what is to what shall be. In this journey we move from one degree of hope to the next because of the work of the Holy Spirit in our lives.

The core of Jesus' message about the reign of God can be found in the Sermon on the Mount—his essential description of covenant love. Christians, and non-Christians too (like Mahatma Gandhi), have found the substance and spirit for their hope in this sermon. This amazing sermon expresses the

12. E. Stanley Jones develops the idea of Christlikeness in nearly all his books, but especially in *Growing Spiritually*, where he uses the fruit of the Spirit to define Christlikeness. He also explores this theme in his book *In Christ*, where he traces the phrase "in Christ" through the New Testament.

13. E. Stanley Jones has written about this extensively, but particularly in his books *Abundant Living* and *The Unshakable Kingdom*.

core values of Christian hope because it testifies boldly to the triumph of love—God's and ours (Matt 5:48).[14] Through this sermon Jesus sought to proclaim and inspire a new humanity, a new community of hope in which the message of love sweeps across the whole world, healing division and restoring life.

Jesus makes it very plain in this sermon that hope will continue to be incarnate in those who choose to follow him. The shalom of God fleshed out in Jesus will continue to find full expression in his disciples.[15] The Beatitudes, in particular, describe the lives of Christians, with each statement offering a unique aspect of hope.

- Those who are "poor in spirit" reveal that hope does not have to be defined and directed by egotism and ethnocentrism.

- Those who are "mournful" instill hope because they demonstrate that those with hard hearts will not prevail.

- Those who are "meek" offer the hope that we can live under God's control.

- Those who "hunger and thirst for righteousness" engender hope through their recognition that we can trust God to care for all our needs.

- Those who are "merciful" reveal that others experience hope whenever we show to others the goodness that God has shown to us.

---

14. Jones, *The Christ of the Mount.*

15. In the book *The Beatitudes of Peace*, John Dear interprets each of the Beatitudes in relation to peacemaking.

- Those who are "pure in heart" demonstrate that living purposefully for God alone produces a hope-filled life.

- Those who are "peacemakers" draw us into the hope of a new creation where the kingdom comes on earth as it is in heaven.

- Those who endure "persecution" inspire a hope that gives us strength to love.

Having laid this foundation in blessedness, the rest of Jesus' sermon expands his vision of what a hope-filled life looks like. His own life and ministry serve, then, to demonstrate that hopeful living is both realistic and attainable.

Jesus' incarnation of God's original vision became the continuing vision of the early church. Jesus transmitted this vision to the first Christians before he ascended into heaven. The forty-day period between his resurrection and his ascension was a time, Luke tells us, when Jesus appeared to the disciples, speaking to them about the kingdom (Acts 1:3). And on his final meeting with them, he instructed them to bear witness to this vision—this message of living hope—in Jerusalem, Judea, Samaria, and to the ends of the earth (Acts 1:8). After Pentecost, they took his words literally and went everywhere, living the message of the kingdom and inviting others to do so as well. Through the person and work of the Holy Spirit in and through the disciples, the risen Jesus became what E. Stanley Jones called "the Christ of every road."[16]

---

16. Jones, *The Christ of Every Road*. This was Jones's third book, a study of Pentecost as the means by which the gospel became present and active in everyone and everything.

St. Paul's Vision of Hope

St. Paul soon entered the picture and did the same thing, making the kingdom of God the essence of his message and summarizing it in the words "righteousness, peace, and joy in the Holy Spirit" (Rom 14:17). Righteousness defines the character of kingdom living. Peace describes the essence of the shalom we encountered in the Old Testament. Joy denotes the countenance of life in God's rule. All three characteristics of life in Christ inspire living hope.

Some of the most powerful words about hope came from St. Paul's pen. While the term *hope* pervades his many letters to the early churches, he seems to have had a particular interest in reminding the Christians in Rome about the gift and importance of hope:

> Endurance produces character, and character produces hope, and hope does not disappoint us, because God's love has been poured into our hearts through the Holy Spirit that has been given to us. (5:4–5 NRSV)

> For in hope we were saved. Now hope that is seen is not hope. For who hopes for what is seen? But if we hope for what we do not see, we wait for it with patience. (8:24–25 NRSV)

> Rejoice in hope, be patient in suffering, persevere in prayer. (12:12 NRSV)

> For whatever was written in former days was written for our instruction, so that by steadfastness and by the encouragement of the scriptures we might have hope. (15:4 NRSV)

> May the God of hope fill you with all joy and peace in believing, so that you may abound in hope by the power of the Holy Spirit. (15:13 NRSV)

In his correspondence with the community of faith in Corinth, he also connected hope directly to faith and love. The church came to refer to these as the theological virtues, but this did not relegate these lofty words to the realm of ideas only. Rather, faith, hope, and love are theological virtues because they lead us into the very nature of God and cultivate those very qualities in our lives.[17] Scholars have viewed the three words as a unity, with love being supreme, giving faith its fire and light to hope.[18] In the New Testament, hope serves as a window word, enabling us to see more clearly into the nature of God and into our own nature. Hope enables us to perceive and embrace the glory of God (Rom 5:2), God's intention to affect our salvation (2 Cor 1:10), our resurrection from the dead (Acts 23:6), our assurance of eternal life (Titus 1:2), and our confidence in Christ's return (1 Pet 1:13).[19]

God's Restoration of Hope

Great as these revelations from Scripture are, the fact is, we do not see the triumph of hope or its pervasive presence in life today. So, the Bible's revelations about hope include an ultimate, culminating vision of hope restored. The term *new creation* epitomizes this vision. The Bible foresees a time when the kingdoms of this world become the kingdom of our Lord and of his Christ (Rev 11:15). This culmination of hope includes both personal and cosmic dimensions. Hope assures us that our lives

17. *Catechism of the Catholic Church*, para. 1812.

18. Barclay, *Letters to the Corinthians*, 140.

19. This summary is spelled out in greater detail by Barclay in *New Testament Words*, 72–76.

are of sacred worth, and through the work of the Spirit we are inspired to connect ever more deeply with the innate goodness (*imago dei*) that is in us. Some have described this as becoming what we already are. Thomas Merton wrote about this and said, "Hope offers the substance of all theology to the individual soul."[20] He is not talking about a privatized, "me-and-Jesus" spirituality; rather, he emphasizes that everything God has in mind for the world, God has in mind for you. Merton calls this the hope of "God's glory revealed in ourselves."[21]

Hope energizes our faith and keeps us pressing on to the higher call of God in Christ Jesus (Phil 3:14). It prevents us from adopting a graduation mentality, where we deceive ourselves into thinking that, at some point, we have everything we need, becoming satisfied and inactive thereafter. Instead, hope keeps us going on to perfection, as John Wesley described it, knowing that in our relationship with an infinite God we can always take another step in faith. Hope also energizes our love, further developing each fruit of the Spirit in relation to our care of and ministry to others. On this profoundly personal level, hope culminates in a comprehensive influence on our character and conduct. Merton associates this influence of hope in our individual lives with the phrase we pray in the Lord's Prayer: "thy kingdom come, thy will be done on earth, as it is in heaven" (Matt 6:10 KJV).

When we embrace hope as individuals, we launch the little boats of our lives into the larger stream of God's reign that the Bible calls a new heaven and a new earth. We cannot realize the

20. Merton, *No Man Is an Island*, 22.
21. Merton, *No Man is an Island*, 23.

promise of hope fully here on earth. There are dimensions of it that await us in heaven. Because of this, some Christians (like E. Stanley Jones, for example) believe that we will continue to grow in eternity. When set free from the limitations of time and space, the impetus of hope knows no end.

The book of Revelation essentially describes the culmination of hope in two acts orchestrated by God: the displacement of all that harms, causes pain, and kills (darkness) with all that inspires good, brings joy, and gives life (light). When John was caught up in this cosmic, heavenly vision, he was filled with hope, and all he could do was cry out to God with a plea for this to happen soon (Rev 22:20). The fact that two thousand years have intervened since John experienced this vision does not diminish our hope. Goodness, joy, life, and hope do not follow a predictable timetable. More often than not, God surprises us with the gift of living hope. That gift comes from the One who said, "I am coming soon," and you can trust that God will bring to pass all that God has promised.

The Magnificence of Living Hope

We have explored wonderful things in the biblical vision of hope. Even so, we have only scratched the surface of everything Scripture has to say about hope. What we have seen, however, brings us back to the insight of Henri Nouwen that we referred to earlier in the chapter—that we live with hope because of the promises of God. Our hope is not concocted out of naiveté; it is constructed on great and precious promises (2 Pet 1:4). God's promises motivate us to be people of hope who offer hope to others until Christ returns.

Any attempt to summarize the biblical message of hope will fall short of its magnitude and magnificence. But an apt description of it comes to us in the word *justice*. When we hear this word today, we quickly connect it to a regulatory mindset and the judicial process. But in both the Old and New Testaments it means more than this.[22] At its base, justice connotes an environment where fairness, equity, and inclusiveness prevail. In the Judeo-Christian tradition this means a comprehensive commitment to the welfare of all, with a particular sensitivity to the poor, oppressed, and marginalized. Justice is essentially love in action. In the Old Testament we see it in the covenantal concern for refugees, immigrants, orphans, and widows. In the New Testament we see the same concern elevated in the full inclusion of Gentiles in the church. The message of hope culminates in the vision of a community in which no one is excluded. This on-earth reality is a precursor to John's vision of heaven where people from every nation, tribe, people, and language celebrate life with God (Rev 7:9). The greatest evidence that the gospel is in effect is that those who are most ignored and vulnerable are given hope.

In our day, we have no greater advocate for hope than Pope Francis. From the very first day of his pontificate he has been an ambassador of hope. Even before he was elected pope, Jorge Mario Bergoglio was known for his theology of hope, connecting it with the virtue of humility and commending it as the spirit that ought to pervade the church. After his election, in his

22. Walter Brueggemann writes about the larger aspects of justice in chapter 6 of his book *A Gospel of Hope*. He uses the word "neighborliness" to describe this constellation of images and views justice as enacting the second great commandment to love our neighbors as ourselves.

first encyclical, *Lumen Fidei*, he wrote extensively about how the light of faith gives hope to the world and how the church is called to be a light-bearer in the world.[23] In a recently published interview with the pope about evangelization, he emphasizes the fact that no person or group should be denied hope or deemed unworthy of it.[24] In this regard, he makes a radical and courageous witness that honors Christ. He stands over against ultra-conservative clergy and laity whom he oversees in the Roman Church, as well as others elsewhere in the body of Christ. He persists in this witness, nonetheless, knowing that he is proclaiming the gospel. He will be remembered as a prophet and pastor of biblical hope.

The witness to living hope in Scripture begins in the opening verses of the Bible and continues all the way through to its final pages. As you journey through this grand narrative, the biblical witness to hope seems to pick up speed. It casts out a large net to include everyone and everything. We are all caught up in it, and we are all called to pass it on.

Discussion

1. Have any of the Scripture passages identified in this chapter reawakened hope in your own life? Which aspect of hope from Scripture speaks most directly to you?

---

23. Pope Francis's *Open Mind, Faithful Heart* is a compilation of sermons he preached before becoming pope.

24. Valente, *Without Him.*

2. Thinking about your church and community, what aspects of the biblical vision of hope come immediately to your mind? Where do you see hope? If you have been a spectator to these testimonies of hope, how might you become an active participant?

3. Are there particular aspects of biblical hope that seem to be most absent in your church and community? What can you do to help rediscover a more robust witness to hope?

4. As you think about your own life, what elements of living hope do you want to cultivate in the days ahead?

TWO
THE LEGACY ABOUT HOPE

At his weekly general audience on May 17, 2017, Pope Francis reflected on Mary Magdalene's meeting with Jesus at the empty tomb—that first exchange of anyone with the risen Lord.[1] "And so that woman," he exclaimed, "now becomes *the apostle of the new and greatest hope.*" Something happened to Mary at the moment of her deepest agony and her darkest despair. "At the time of tears and abandonment," the pope continued, "she hears the Risen Jesus who calls us by name, and with a heart full of joy goes to announce: I have seen the Lord!" Pope Francis has referred to Mary as the apostle of hope ever since, aligning her equally with another who shares that title—the apostle Paul. Mary became part of a story much bigger than herself. The signs of hope that define our future are rooted in the narratives of hope that fill our past.[2]

Thank goodness we don't have to manufacture hope; rather, our remembrance of the stories that have shaped us draws us into a hope-filled future. We have inherited an amazing legacy about hope. While hope may not be based on what we can see

1. Pope Francis, "Papal Audience of 17 May 2017."
2. This is one of the central themes that pervades President Barack Obama's best-selling book, *The Audacity of Hope.*

in the present, the past offers an infinite number of inspiring and encouraging stories of hope. These stories alone could fill volumes. They buoy us up in the midst of our own personal quests for hope. They encourage communities to look up and out—to plant seeds of hope—when injustice robs the vulnerable and marginalized of joy and steals their dreams. When we forget who we are and what we are called to be and do, we rediscover our identity through the gift of hope. Our forebears in the faith have demonstrated the power of hope time and time again.

No one can escape tragedy in life. But some of the most catastrophic situations end in hope. When despair has beaten people into the ground, hope has lifted them up. We have seen it. Not even death can vanquish hope. When life ends—when everything seems to fall to our feet in ashes—hope for new possibilities brings forth new life. Hope, we say, springs eternal. In the face of injustice, we have caught glimpses of a just world because of hope. Hope resuscitates those who need life breathed back into them. This is equally true of churches as it is of individuals. Hope is like a space in which we reside. Being in a dark, despairing place is excruciating. But our personal memory and the larger memory of the community of faith declares to each of us that we do not need to live in that space. Hope resituates us into a space of shalom. The practice of remembering feeds this hope. We tend to forget. But we find hope in our memory—in the legacy about hope that surrounds us on every side.

The witness of God's people in history restores our hope in the face of tragedy and despair, injustice and evil, spiritual amnesia and malaise, and through the power of song and sacrament.

Hope in the Face of Tragedy and Despair

Tragedy happens. Natural disasters lead to untold suffering and despair. People lose hope. Unfortunately, the actions of human beings and nations also lead to cataclysmic situations that plunge us into despair. In human history, nothing has produced more misery and anguish than war. The two World Wars of the previous century nearly depleted hope entirely in the Western world. But a poignant story illustrates how, even in the midst of such despair, the simple act of a faithful couple had the power to restore hope.

You may recognize the name Jürgen Moltmann, a name synonymous with the "theology of hope." Paul first met Professor Moltmann when he was a graduate student at Duke University. During one of the professor's visits to campus, he invited him to lunch and they enjoyed a wonderful meal together. While introducing himself more fully, Paul explained that he was working in his doctoral studies with Frank Baker. "Oh," Moltmann interrupted, "I'd like to share a story with you about Frank and Nellie Baker."

During World War II there was a German prisoner of war camp on the northeast coast of England near the city of Hull. A young pastor and his wife served a small Methodist circuit close by. They were filled with compassion and compelled to do something to reach out to the German prisoners who were their neighbors. They went to the commander and asked permission to take a prisoner with them to church each Sunday and then to their home where they would eat their Sunday dinner together. It was agreed. Sunday after Sunday, a steady flow of German soldiers worshiped and ate with the Bakers in their home throughout the course of the war. This world-famous theologian paused, looked at Paul intently, and said, "One of those soldiers was a young man by the name of Jürgen Moltmann, and it was at Frank and Nellie Baker's dinner table that the seed of hope was planted in my heart." Hope is often fragile because life is fragile, but a simple act of kindness or hospitality can fan a flickering flame into a living hope.

In our own time, perhaps nothing has brought greater despair than the pandemic of HIV/AIDS. In Africa, in particular, this disease has ravaged entire communities, leaving none behind but the very young and the very old. In Rwanda, the horrible genocide of 1994 exacerbated this scourge. Thousands of children found themselves without parents, attempting to fend for themselves and surviving family members. ZOE Ministry responded to the plight of these children with programs under the umbrella of "Giving Hope." These hope-bearers sought to empower orphans and vulnerable children to provide for themselves and grow into the men and women God would have them be—physically, socially, mentally, and spiritually. The goal of what is now ZOE Empowers continues to be the empowerment of orphans with the hope that they will all realize their full potential.[3]

---

3. ZOE Empowers, an Advance Special of the United Methodist General Board of Global Ministries, currently operates in six nations (Kenya, Rwanda, Zimbabwe, Malawi, Liberia, and India) with nearly forty-five thousand empowered children in nearly five hundred empowerment groups. For more information and ways to support this ministry, see https://zoeempowers.org/.

Jean was a vulnerable Rwandan child in a seemingly hopeless situation. Having lost both his parents, he struggled to provide for himself and his three siblings, including a sister with disabilities. He was devastated by grief and racked by guilt because of his inability to provide for his younger siblings. ZOE staff discovered him living on the streets and eking out an existence on scraps picked from the garbage. Jean was immediately welcomed into an empowerment group with other orphaned children. The leader asked him to think about his future using a practice called the "dream process." This involves drawing a picture of your life dream. Jean sketched it out and, as a consequence of that simple act, you could see the spark of hope return to his face and begin to shine in his eyes. ZOE demonstrated to him that he had a loving, heavenly Father and a new family upon which to depend. In less than two years, Jean achieved complete self-sufficiency, caring for his siblings properly in his own home, developing a thriving farm business, evangelizing his community, and paying forward all he received to other orphans. Drawn by the testimony of his joyful life, others are still flocking to Jean to discover the secret of the hope he exudes.

In the midst of tragedy and despair, God uses the community of faith to restore hope and transform lives.

Hope in the Face of Injustice and Evil

Elie Wiesel, a holocaust survivor of great renown, opened his Nobel Peace Prize lecture on "Hope, Despair, and Memory" with an ancient Hasidic legend. In a time of great evil and injustice, a rabbi known as the Besht was stripped of all his special powers. He and his servant were banished to a distant island where they wept together. Abandoned and overwhelmed by their despair, both men forgot everything. The Besht could not even remember how to pray. Ultimately, the only thing that his servant could remember was the alphabet. The Besht asked the servant to help him remember it as well. So the two began to recite the alphabet together. Over and over again they named the letters that gave their language shape. Each time more vigorously, more fervently, until ultimately, the Besht regained his powers, having regained his memory. "Without memory, our existence would be barren and opaque, like a prison cell into which no light penetrates; like a tomb which rejects the living," Wiesel reflected. "Memory saved the Besht, and if anything can, it is memory that will save humanity. For me, hope without memory is like memory without hope."

Magda Herzberger was born in a small Romanian village just three hours south of Wiesel's hometown. Like him, she survived the terrors of Nazism, offering us a compelling story of hope. On April 18, 1944, Nazi sympathizers herded her and her parents—and other Jewish neighbors—onto trucks bound for a ghetto that served as a staging area for deportations to the death camps. As she explains in her biographical account of those years, *Survivor*, she served as a corpse gatherer, resisted the lure of suicide, and relied on God for the hope to outlive the Nazi death machine. She says that she always had a deep, abiding sense in her innermost being that God would help her make it out alive. Her greatest gift has been helping young people experience grace and discover hope in the darkest of places. She identifies her great trust in God as the source of her survival.

Regardless of what she experienced in the camps—all those atrocities meant to dehumanize her and destroy her hopes and dreams—she was still able to love and forgive. She describes this as the greatest miracle of all. This miracle makes her story a story of hope.

Hope, however, did not come easily to Magda. It did not raise her *above* her tribulations. In her biography she recounts how her hope was forged *in* the crucible of her suffering. For more than twenty years, regular nightmares and depression plagued her nights and days. Eventually, writing poetry liberated her from the prison created by the brutality and injustice she experienced. In her poems she explores the unconscious trauma of her vivid dreams. It was not until the 1990s that she challenged herself to write about her experiences in the concentration camps. By that time, her desire to tell her story had become so strong that nothing could prevent her from doing so. She concludes her biography with these poignant words: "There is always a twilight and a new dawn. Day is followed by night and night is followed by day. A resurrection takes place within us each day. We remember the past, it belongs to us; and yet, we have to learn from the past so that we can grow in the future. After the dark night there is daybreak."[4]

We capture glimpses of hope from stories like this. Hope breaks in upon us as these narratives remind us about God's vision of a new creation. God surprises us with hope, sometimes when we least expect to find it. God breaks through the injustice and evil in our world to offer glimpses of hope through signs of shalom.

---

4. Herzberger, *Survival*, 367.

Hope in the Face of Spiritual Amnesia & Malaise

Throughout the course of its history, the church has fallen prey to forces that leave it weak, vulnerable, and in need of renewal. The famous phrase *ecclesia semper reformanda* can be translated roughly, "the church is always in need of reform." There have been periods, though, when things were unbelievably bleak. You would wonder how the church could ever survive the conflicts on the outside and the fears on the inside. In moments of spiritual amnesia and malaise, tension and division, people in the church lose hope. Movements like monasticism in the late medieval period and the various awakenings of the eighteenth century reveal the cycle of renewal in the life of the church.

As the so-called medieval "age of faith" began to crumble under the weight of its own "successes," new movements of spiritual awakening began to emerge. They cut through the layers of power and authority in the church to birth a new sense of religious freedom. In these movements, vital spirituality displaced a fixation on the institutions of the church. A women's movement known as the Beguines stood at the forefront of these developments.[5] Essentially these were pious women who chose to lead communal lives of prayer and service, first founding their communities in the twelfth century in the Netherlands and Belgium. Their vision was simple. Focus on the person of Jesus. Read the Bible. Follow your heart. Pursue holiness.

A monastic pattern of prayer and devotion provided the "spiritual rhythm" of these women's houses or Beguinages. In

---

5. In her study of *Beguine Spirituality*, Fiona Bowie describes this as the first great women's movement in Europe.

contrast to the convents of the day that catered to the needs of the gentry and nobility, they reserved their teaching for those children who were marginalized and deprived of education. This led to large numbers of resident children and orphans in many of the homes. According to Fiona Bowie, a 1646 census of the Great Beguinage in Leuven revealed "a total of 272 children living in about sixty different houses (out of a total of around a hundred), the number of children exceeding that of beguines."[6] The Beguines were known, more than anything else, for restoring hope to the hopeless.

At the beginning of the eighteenth century in England, seismic demographic and cultural shifts led to a monumental deflation of hope among the masses of the poor. William Hogarth, a contemporary printmaker and pictorial satirist, provides a window into the desperate conditions of life in England's urban centers. His print entitled "Gin Lane" depicts the disastrous consequences of alcohol abuse with heartrending scenes of starvation, riot, and suicide. He levels a scathing indictment against the church because of the way in which it had abandoned the poor. He lambasted the apathy and aloofness of the Christian community. "The Sleeping Congregation" portrays a typical parish church with its snoring congregants and dishonorable clergy. The church he portrays wreaks of irrelevance. The church was failing to be the church.

The Wesleyan tradition arose from within the Church of England as a movement of spiritual renewal.[7] John and Charles Wesley, who gave leadership to this revival that bore their name,

6. Bowie, *Beguine Spirituality*, 26.

7. The Wesleyan tradition as a movement of renewal in the church continues to invite thoughtful studies. See Chilcote, *The Wesleyan Tradition*.

were loyal priests within the church. They dedicated their lives to the rediscovery of what they called "primitive" or "scriptural Christianity." In a sermon published late in his life, John Wesley proclaimed: "How great a thing it is to be a Christian, to be a real, inward, scriptural Christian! Conformed in heart and life to the will of God!"[8] His primary concern was to do all he could to help realize God's vision for every person and for our world. He enabled his followers to discover their true identity as the children of God. He empowered them for ministry by providing means for them to uncover their giftedness and to grow in grace. Charles Wesley helped them sing this vision and the hope it instilled into being. The quest of the Wesley brothers was for Christian wholeness, for holiness of heart and life, for faith working by love.

The Wesleys invested their time and energy among those who lived under the cloud of hopelessness. Instead of waiting for people to come to them, they took the good news of God's love to them wherever they were. Women, in particular, who were sidelined and ignored, responded enthusiastically. Hester Ann Rogers felt distant from God. Her journal details the interior tensions and the external obstacles that left her hopeless. She was simply unable to find rest in God. Then she came under the ministry of the Methodist community. "The heavens appeared as brass and hope seemed almost sunk into despair," she writes, "when suddenly the Lord spoke those words to my heart, 'Believe on the Lord Jesus Christ, and thou shalt be saved.' That word came with divine evidence and sweetness to my heart, 'Cast all thy care upon him, for he careth for thee.'"[9]

8. Wesley, "On a Single Eye," in *Sermons IV*, 121.
9. Quoted in Chilcote, *Early Methodist Spirituality*, 106.

That day, God filled her with hope. It is not too much to say that the Methodists poured hope into the lives of those forgotten by the church. "My little vessel is as full as it can hold, and I would pour out all that fullness before Thee, that my heart may become capable of receiving more and more," Isabella Wilson prayed. "Thou art my hope, and help, and salvation."[10] Quoting a Charles Wesley hymn, her soul cried out, "My hope is full, O glorious hope!"[11]

"Fresh Expressions of Church," and other semi-monastic movements similar to the Beguines and the early Methodists, are helping spiritual wanderers and seekers find hope anew today. We believe that movements of inclusive love are spreading throughout the church. In the face of religious exclusivity they are rediscovering Jesus' radical way of inclusion. Even when the church flounders and struggles, God finds a way to restore hope.

Hope in Song & Sacrament

In 1708 Isaac Watts published a lyrical paraphrase of Psalm 90. The opening lines of his well-known hymn aptly express the central theme of this chapter: "O God, our help in ages past / Our hope for years to come." Perhaps nothing has inspired hope among God's people more than the songs they have sung. Likewise, nothing induces hope more fully than the community of faith gathered together around God's inclusive Table of thanksgiving.

10. Quoted in Chilcote, *Her Own Story*, 63.
11. Quoted in Chilcote, *Early Methodist Spirituality*, 133.

The songs we sing do not have to include the word "hope" in order to lift us up into that space of shalom. George Matheson knew the despair of heartache and loneliness. He excelled in his studies at Glasgow University, but learned before his education was even completed that he was going blind rapidly. Moreover, he had met and fallen in love with a fellow student who, when learning about his condition, said that she did not want to marry a blind man. He was devastated. Years later, on the evening of his sister's wedding, that rejection came flooding back and threw him into a deep depression. He recalls what happened next:

> The hymn was the fruit of that suffering. It was the quickest bit of work I ever did in my life. I had the impression of having it dictated to me by some inward voice rather than of working it out myself. I am quite sure that the whole work was completed in five minutes, and equally sure that it never received at my hands any retouching or correction. I have no natural gift of rhythm. All the other verses I have ever written are manufactured articles; this came like a dayspring from on high.[12]

Here are some of the words he wrote:

> O love that will not let me go,
> I rest my weary soul in thee;
> I give thee back the life I owe,
> That in thine ocean depths its flow
> May richer, fuller be.
>
> O joy that seekest me through pain,
> I cannot close my heart to thee;
> I chase the rainbow through the rain,
> And feel the promise is not vain
> That morn shall tearless be.

12. Hawn, "History of Hymns: 'O Love That Wilt Not Let Me Go.'"

With his hope restored, he later entered the ministry of the church, earning an honorary Doctor of Divinity degree from the University of Edinburgh for his many contributions to the spiritual vitality of the community of faith.

In a devotional work entitled *Adventures for the Soul* (1987), Natalie Sleeth described some of her most significant compositions, including her best-known creation, "Hymn of Promise." According to Sleeth, a T. S. Eliot line—"in our end is our beginning"—provided the germ of inspiration for this hymn with its hope-filled opening line, "In the bulb there is a flower." She composed this hymn when she was "pondering the ideas of life, death, spring and winter, Good Friday and Easter, and the whole reawakening of the world that happens every spring."[13] Her husband, having been diagnosed with cancer, requested that this hymn be sung at his funeral. This hymn celebrates the freedom of the butterfly that emerges from the hidden promise of the cocoon. Sleeth reminds us that even in our doubt there is believing. Despite the fact that our lives are finite, we experience eternity in the here and now. Only God can see those glorious promises yet unrevealed. But in our death we experience resurrection; at the last, we taste victory. The singer celebrates a magnificent anticipation of new life and hope.

Nothing inspires hope more than actually singing about hope itself, and no one has given us a more powerful hymn for this purpose than Georgia Harkness. She based the text of "Hope of the World" on the theme of the Second Assembly of the World Council of Churches, meeting in Evanston in August 1954—"Jesus Christ, Hope of the World." The Hymn Society

13. Sleeth, *Adventures for the Soul*, 36.

selected her hymn as the theme song for the event and it was first sung at the opening session of the Assembly. She composed this hymn in the wake of World War II and the Korean Conflict and in the midst of a "Cold War" that threatened the future. The Christ of great compassion, she claims, is the hope of the world. She prays for him to speak to the hearts of those who are consumed by false hopes. She describes Jesus—the hope of the world—as God's gift from highest heaven. We place our hope in him because he is the only one who can heal our wounds and end our bitter strife. The hope we have in Jesus saves us from death and dark despair. Harkness boldly proclaims that Christians find their hope in Christ, who is the hope of the whole human family.

Whenever we gather around the Table to celebrate Eucharist, we bring the whole human community into our hearts and minds as well. Participation in the Lord's Supper infuses hope into our souls. Hope, in fact, was one of the keynotes in the early Methodist celebrations of Holy Communion. Charles Wesley viewed the sacrament as an anticipation of that great heavenly banquet, characterized by joy, peace, and love. The amazing imagery of his hymns reflects a vision of the church as a community of hope with arms wide open to all:

> How glorious is the life above
> Which in this ordinance we *taste*;
> That fullness of celestial love,
> That joy which shall forever last!
>
> Sure pledge of ecstasies unknown
> Shall this divine communion be,
> The ray shall rise into a sun,
> The drop shall swell into a sea.[14]

14. Wesley, *Hymns on the Lord's Supper*, 87.

The poignant story of a Latin American Methodist leader illustrates concretely the way in which Eucharist restores hope. During a period of horrendous oppression on the part of his government, he and many of the members of his congregation found themselves in prison on an Easter Sunday morning. Many within their community had been killed and many of them feared for their own lives. Despite the fact that they had no provisions for a celebration of Holy Communion, they sang resurrection hymns together, prayed, and the pastor led them through the liturgy. When it came time to consecrate the elements, he elevated his empty hands and said: "The bread which we do not have today is a reminder of those who are hungry, for those who are oppressed, and for those who yearn for the provision that only God can give."

After consecrating the bread, he took a virtual cup in his hands and said: "The wine which we do not have today is a reminder of those who, with Jesus, have shed their blood for the sake of righteousness. Through their sacrifice, they join with Jesus in witness to the triumph of God's love over all those forces that seek to destroy life. Through our participation in this sacred meal we promise to seek righteousness, justice, and peace in all we do." The Eucharist re-forms the church—the community of God's faithful people. It fills them with hope. It provides an opportunity for them to recommit themselves to God's will and God's way. The community then moves from the Table into the world to proclaim and live God's vision of shalom—inclusivity and love for all.[15]

15. Cited in Chilcote, "Eucharist and Formation," 192–93.

Ghanaian Methodists in West Africa have a wonderful tradition of receiving the elements of Holy Communion at the exits of the church as they depart to serve. They receive their food for the journey, as it were, and are filled not only with bread but with hope. God restores hope in our lives as we gather around the Table and are sent out into God's world in mission. This sacred meal gives us reason to hope.

Discussion

1. When you have found yourself in a place of despair, what stories of faith have helped reawaken hope in your own life? What was it about these stories that inspired hope?

2. What are the forces conspiring to foster despair in our world and your community today? How do these developments affect you and what can you do to foster hope among those around you?

3. Are there particular hymns or sacred songs that lift your spirits when you are down—that restore your hope? Reflect on a particular time when singing your faith restored your hope.

4. Meals, and our family meal—Eucharist—in particular, have the power to instill hope in the community of faith. Reflect on an experience of the sacrament in which you were lifted above your circumstances and resituated in a "space of shalom."

THREE

THE REASON FOR HOPE

The age in which we live feels hopeless to so many. God calls us to a living hope today in the face of monumental challenges, to say the least. And so many indicators point to the conclusion that this will not end soon. It is no exaggeration to say that we are living in a time when hope is in short supply. Reflecting on what seems to be a dire situation, Martin Marty has observed: "If you pay even marginal attention to media, politics, arts and yes, religion, you may have noticed the near disappearance, or, one hopes, merely the eclipse of hope in our culture of prevalent hopelessness."[1] We agree with Dr. Marty—we feel this ourselves—and we have written this book with the hope that it might contribute to a much-needed revival of hope now.

But we are not the first people to feel this way. In fact, the first Christians lived at a time in which it was hard to hope. St. Peter told his brothers and sisters in the faith, "Whenever anyone asks you to speak of your hope, be ready to defend it" (1 Pet 3:15). Why did he need to do that? Because in challenging times, many believe that we conjure up hope simply as a way

1. Marty, "Revived 'Theology of Hope.'"

of avoiding reality. From a biblical perspective, however, living realistically requires the disposition of living hope. We, like St. Peter, must defend hope against those who would lure us to abandon it at the very time we need it the most. The Christian message is rooted in hope, and we have reasons for the hope that lies within us. Even reflecting together on some of the reasons for hope can instill a living hope in our lives. Here are six reasons for hope upon which we invite your reflections.

Hope as a Life Orientation

First and foremost, hope is a total life orientation. It is not an isolated part of life; it is the organizing principle around which all life revolves. It's presence or absence determines what the substance of our life will be and what shape it will take. Parker Palmer spoke about this in an *On Being* interview. "Hope keeps me alive," he claimed, "and creatively engaged in the world."[2] Vaclav Havel wrote similarly, distinguishing hope from optimism by describing hope as a nexus where life "above and below" converge. He expanded this image:

> I think that the deepest and most important form of hope, the only one that can keep us above water and urge us to good works, and the only true source of the breathtaking dimension of the human spirit and its efforts, is something we get, as it were, from "elsewhere." It is also this hope, above all which gives us strength to live and continually to try new things, even in conditions that seem as hopeless as ours do, here and now.[3]

2. Palmer, "Hope Is the Place."
3. Havel, "An Orientation of the Heart," 82–83.

Havel's poignant words call us into a vision of hope that reflects both the divine and the human—a vision that informs and empowers our words and deeds in every area of life. In the same *On Being* interview noted above, Parker Palmer put it this way: "Hope is the place where joy meets the struggle." Living hope resides in the heart, in the very center of our vocation in life. Similarly, Frederic Buechner defines vocation as "the place where your deep gladness and the world's deep hunger meet."[4]

Hope as a total life orientation reveals one of the most basic questions about living hope, "How is my life and my work an opportunity to give a reason for hope and offer hope to others?" No one can answer that question for you. The answer arises from the work you do each day. Buechner points out that your work is most truly vocational in nature when you bring joy to those things that simply need to be done—those daily actions that need to be done for the sake of the world.[5] Giving the reason for our hope, in other words, begins, continues, and ends in the everyday routines, in the little things, of our lives.

Hope as a Mark of Faith

Second, as an orientation of the heart, hope is a mark of faith. The writer of the Letter to the Hebrews understood this, defining faith as "the reality of what we hope for" (Heb 11:1). But what does that mean? The question is not easy to answer, for we are so accustomed (particularly in the West) to defining reality in terms of things that are already present. The affirmation of the writer of Hebrews moves us into a different mindset—that

4. Buechner, *Wishful Thinking*, 95.
5. Buechner, *Wishful Thinking*, 95.

is, the recognition that Reality is always breaking in to the present, as Havel said, "from elsewhere."

Hope is a mark of faith precisely because it will not allow us to define Reality by the status quo, and surely not by the sacred cows we breed to give primary value to secondary things. Faith is the reality of what we hope for because it is the openness we must exhibit if we are to grow into maturity as Christians in ways that are both deep and wide. Without hope, faith deteriorates into certitude, and once we are "certain," we not only cease to grow, we erect barriers to keep new thoughts at bay and bunkers to inhabit against those whom we allege to be enemies of truth. With hope, we live unafraid. We are willing to take our convictions into the marketplace of ideas, knowing that those convictions which are of God will endure and those which are not will pass away and/or evolve into greater truth.

Hope as a Creative Energy

This leads directly to a third aspect of living hope as a creative energy. Because hope creates openness, we allow it to set a trajectory into the future. Without apology we say, "I believe," but we do not allow our beliefs to become brittle. Rather, we express them in a larger context of construction. When E. Stanley Jones was asked if he was a Christian, he almost always answered, "I am a Christian under construction." He knew that he could never exhaust or come to the end of an infinite God. Hope kept the door open to the future and ignited an energy in him which allowed him to speak of the best years of his life as "the next ten." Even after suffering a major stroke, he continued to give a reason for the hope that was in him—a hope established by the risen Christ, whom Brother Stanley called "The Divine Yes," using St. Paul's words to do so (2 Cor 1:19–20).[6] Jones stands alongside similar exemplars over the centuries, witnesses who discovered that hope was a critical, creative energy in their lives. Dorothy Day surely stands among them. The length, depth, and breadth of her work—combined with the resistance she received—bear witness to the flame of hope that ever burned in her heart. Like the rest of us, it sometimes burned low. But it never completely went out. She found it rekindled over and over through the community of faith, speaking of the church as "the place flooded with sunshine"—a place of hope.[7] But even the church was only the container of something more magnificent, the glory and majesty of God. She bore witness to it using the words of St. Dionysius, describing the Godhead as "the Cause and Origin and Being and Life of all creation."[8]

With respect to hope, this meant that Dorothy carried a vision of "something more"—something finer and more sacred—than any moment could contain. That vision energized her life, not only reminding her that she was God's beloved child, but that everyone else was as well! Hope was the vision that enabled her to see Christ in herself but also to see Christ in others, writing that it was "through such exercise that we grow, and the joy of our vocation assures us that we are on the right path."[9] She referred to this assurance as "the grace of hope, this

6. Jones, *The Divine Yes.*

7. Garvey, *Dorothy Day*, 35.

8. Garvey, *Dorothy Day*, 35; a quotation from Dionysius's work entitled *Concerning the Godhead.*

9. Garvey, *Dorothy Day*, 45.

consciousness that there is, in every person, that which is of God."[10] Dorothy Day's reason for hope was an abiding creative energy.

Hope as a Tenacious Reality

A fourth insight emerges from this energy linked with hope: hope as a tenacious reality. Far from being a Pollyanna, "pie-in-the-sky" fragile fantasy, hope is what Martin Luther King Jr. called "the strength to love."[11] Hope provided King's vision—his "dream"—to see the promised land without any assurance that he himself would ever enter it. Nevertheless, he kept showing up so that others could enjoy it one day. Hope moves us with passion to overcome evil with good. It cleans the lens of our vision so that we can see what needs to happen, and it provides us with the willpower to work for change. As a tenacious reality, hope protects us from becoming passive or cynical.

The tenacious reality of living hope brings into action its prophetic dimensions: calling out, calling up, and calling forth.

- Hope calls out by revealing the inadequacy of status quo living, so frequently defined and directed by egotism and ethnocentrism.

- Hope calls up by creating a resistance to that status quo and a resolve to move beyond it.

- Hope calls forth by envisioning the new day of God's reign when the old order passes away and the new comes.

10. Garvey, *Dorothy Day*, 58.
11. See his book of this title.

Walter Brueggemann provides a robust definition of this kind of hope, noting that "hope is not a rational argument or an intellectual exercise. Hope is a bodily engagement with the facts on the ground, the astonishing concrete capacity to work newness by a word, a gesture, an act."[12] The tenacity of hope offers a future different from the present—a transformed future envisioned and realized by those who refuse to stop trusting God. It is the kind of hope the hymnwriter described, "Though the wrong seems oft so strong, / God is the ruler yet."[13]

We are called as the church to be the bearers of tenacious hope. It is this kind of hope that the children of Israel experienced as they fled from Pharaoh and found that "just in time" the waters of the sea parted so that they could make it to the other side. King David described tenacious hope as the means for making it through the valley of the shadow of death (Ps 23:4). Jesus pled for John the Baptist to hold on to hope when he had all but given up on Jesus' messiahship. "Those who were blind are able to see," he acknowledged. "Those who are crippled now walk. People with skin diseases are cleansed. Those who were deaf now hear. Those who were dead are raised up. And good news is preached to the poor" (Luke 7:22). Those who believed saw the fruit of this hope in Jesus, the seeds of which were planted so long before in Isaiah's original prophecy. Jesus enabled John to claim this past/present hope even when it seemed to take so long to materialize.

People come to the church week after week, asking by virtue of their attendance, "Is there any reason for hope?" We

12. Brueggemann, *Tenacious Solidarity*, 178.

13. From the hymn of Maltbie D. Babcock, "This is My Father's World," 144.

have the opportunity to be the "beloved community" that te-
naciously exclaims, "Yes! There is reason for hope." As hope-
bearers, we can be instruments of God's peace to give folks
reason to be hopeful when they scatter from the sanctuary to
serve in the world. God offers us this grand privilege and holy
responsibility.

Hope as a Transforming Dynamic

Whenever this happens, we discover a fifth reason for hope: a
transforming dynamic. Living hope changes people and situations—hope transforms. Things cannot remain the same under
the influence of living hope. But for that to happen several elements must come into play. First, we must be people of courage.
Courage does not mean to rely ultimately on ourselves; rather,
it entails holding fast to our trust in God. According to Parker
Palmer, this kind of hope "is grounded not in our own ability to
solve problems, but in God's love, God's justice, God's promise
of fidelity to us. That promise, as we have seen, is the promise
of reconciliation, a kingdom in which strangers will now themselves be as one."[14]

The lack of any "self-reliance" is what, in fact, makes this
kind of hope courageous. When we rely on ourselves it is not
courage that we manifest, it is presumption. Courageous hope
calls us outside of ourselves into the One who is the source of
hope. To exhibit courageous hope means to be radically and simultaneously humble and assertive. Humility characterizes this

14. Palmer, *Company of Strangers*, 175. Along with others, Palmer has organized this kind of hope into the Center for Courage Renewal. Notice the link
between courage and renewal in the name of this movement.

hope because we never forget from whom it comes; courageous hope requires an assertiveness, however, because it must always be called into actions in some concrete way. This kind of living hope challenges all forms of imperialism because it is rooted in an operative vision of the kingdom of God.

Prophetic resistance brings transformative hope to life. Artist Suzi Gablik rightly notes that art only becomes art when the artist transcends art for its own sake.[15] In great prophetic figures like Mahatma Gandhi, John Dear, and Wil Gafney, we see hope expressed in the ever-flowing stream of nonviolent resistance. Walter Brueggemann calls such prophets "emancipated imaginers of alternatives."[16] He offers a compelling vision of prophetic resistance as a form of art. In order for hope to emerge from such resistance, the prophetic artist must engage God in a contemplative manner—immersing oneself in love. This safeguards proactive resistance that is hope-filled from becoming reactive behavior that can be destructive. James Lawson, a pioneer nonviolent-resistance teacher during the civil rights era, reinforced the contemplative foundation for hopeful activism with this memorable phrase: "We must be still before God prior to being active for God."[17]

This kind of hope-filled resistance is a subversive, not a revolutionary, act. A revolutionary person seeks to change things by standing outside a situation; a subversive person works "on the edge of the inside" to effect change.[18] By posi-

15. In her book *The Re-enchantment of Art*, Suzi Gablik unpacks the ways in which this transformation occurs. In this re-enchantment, art and the artist become social activists for a higher good.

16. Brueggemann, *From Judgment to Hope*, vii–viii.

17. Lawson, "Notes from an Architect of Non-Violence."

18. This is one of Richard Rohr's frequently used phrases to describe the kind of prophetic resistance called for in our day.

tioning ourselves there, we bear witness to the community in two particular ways: 1) that our souls do not belong to "the company store" and 2) that even "the company store" can be different in the future than it is in the present. Only God's grace makes these witnesses possible. From the perspective of Scripture, God is always at work to bring a new creation into being. As ambassadors of hope, we testify to that vision, and we celebrate every incremental movement in the "already/not yet" realization of the kingdom of God.

Hope as a Long Obedience

A sixth reason for hope flows from this transformational dynamic: hope involves a long obedience—a marathon, not a sprint. Vaclav Havel observes that impatient people generate false hope. "They want to see immediate results," he maintains. "Anything that does not produce immediate results seems foolish."[19] True hope, he notes, preserves the correct perspective, that things can only be evaluated years after they take place. Hope as a long obedience is more like a seed than a mature plant—more akin to what is sown than what is reaped.

An old story captures what we are trying to say. A seeker finally made it to a guru to ask what he thought about something which had happened a thousand years ago. Expecting a wise teaching to come from the question, the young seeker was surprised when the guru replied, "I have no thoughts." When asked why, the guru explained, "Because not enough time has elapsed for me to have a perspective."[20] In an age in which speed

19. Havel, "An Orientation of the Heart," 88–89.

20. This story is found in various versions and in different religions. In the

is viewed as a virtue and instant gratification as a right, these words seem foolish. But they are, in fact, the essence of wisdom with respect to hope. The sign that hope lives in and through us is not that we can put check marks against our list of "important things to do," but that we have written down those things in a form that allows them to be handed on to others. Setting the right trajectory, not coming to the end of it, defines hope as a long obedience.

We see this spirit in St. Paul's passing the torch of leadership to Timothy and Titus. We see it in the exhortation of the author of the Letter to the Hebrews to run the race that is set before us—that is, our allotted time on the track—ready to pass the torch to a new generation, and to do so with joy. Living hope requires this long obedience.

Hope and the Eucharistic Feast

In this chapter we have identified and borne witness to reasons why being hopeful is not only a legitimate but also a necessary stance and practice in life. Within the Christian tradition, moreover, we also enact hope in concrete ways—in signs—where all this comes together in poignant ways. We return to Eucharist again as one of those sign-acts of love in which we experience living hope. When we come to the Table, we come to the place where hope reigns supreme. The meal signals to us that grace instills hope in our lives. We come to that place where we view Christ as central to the entire hopeful enterprise, and we proclaim that "Christ has died. Christ is risen. Christ will come

---

Christian tradition it has the parallel of God's sense of time: "A single day is like a thousand years and a thousand years are like a single day" (2 Pet 3:8).

again." All three sentences testify to the reality of hope in the economy of God's love.

When we say, "Christ has died," we are speaking not so much of his physical death, but of his atoning ministry and redemptive work. The cross stands as our most enduring symbol of hope, not despair; a sign of victory, not defeat. The cross confronts us with the loving sacrifice made by Christ for the redemption of the world (Col 1:20). We encounter the cross-shaped pattern—imitating it in our own lives—and thereby opening the possibility for our own sacrifices to be redemptive as well. When we participate with Christ, taking up our own crosses to follow him, these actions offer others Christ's living hope.

When we say, "Christ is risen," we bear witness to the hope that, just as death did not have the last word over Jesus, it does not have the final word over us, over others, or over the world. Resurrection is our word of hope because it is the word of life. Emil Brunner—in his reflections on hope after having lost two sons in their early twenties—provides this memorable analogy: "What oxygen is for the lungs, such is hope for the meaning of human life. . . . Take hope away and humanity is constricted through lack of breath."[21] Hopelessness means death; hope brings new life. And so, St. Peter writes in a triumphant tone, "Blessed be the God and Father of our Lord Jesus Christ! By his great mercy he has given us a new birth into a living hope through the resurrection of Jesus Christ from the dead" (1 Pet 1:3 NRSV).

---

21. Quoted in Brown, *Message of Numbers*, commentary on Num 24:15–25.

When we say "Christ will come again," we are testifying to our hope that there is a divine plan—a holy and ultimate purpose being effected by God. The writer to the community of faith in Ephesus described it in these terms: "This is what God planned for the climax of all times: to bring all things together in Christ, the things in heaven along with the things on earth" (Eph 1:10). Everything moves irresistibly to the Omega Point described by Teilhard de Chardin. In the end (as John saw it in his revelatory vision) every enemy will ultimately be vanquished, and we will dwell in a new heaven and new earth where everyone is illuminated by the Light of God (Rev 21 and 22 unpack this vision). No wonder, then, that we call all this our glorious hope. We "remember" it (reconnect with it and recommit ourselves to it) every time we participate in the Eucharist. This "Holy Mystery" reminds us of the living hope by which we have been saved (past), the living hope into which we are called in the here and now (present), and the living hope toward which we strive as we participate in God's mission of love that yet awaits fulfillment (future).

The basis for our eucharistic hope is gratitude—gratefulness for all that God has done for us in Christ.[22] We return to the Table again and again, and as we do, hope arises from our gratitude because, through the Eucharist we have encountered the God who has begun a good work in us and is at work to bring it to completion at the day of Christ Jesus (Phil 1:6). And what we believe to be true for us, we believe to be true for

22. We are indebted to Brother David Steindl-Rast for his pervasive and instructive teachings about hope. His book *Gratefulness, the Heart of Prayer* is a good place to begin in tracing his theology of gratitude; cf. Butler-Bass, *Grateful*. Interestingly, she uses the word "subversive" to describe the life of gratitude, viewing it similarly to the way we have done earlier in this chapter.

everyone else—a belief that ignites the flame of desire in us to be bearers of the message, in word and deed, as much and as often as we can.

What we have described in this chapter is more than a good, or even moving, idea. It is what Walter Brueggemann calls "an urgent summons."[23] The reasons for our hope must become the foundations for our action. As David Orr rightly notes, "hope is a verb with the sleeves rolled up."[24] In the next chapter we commend specific concrete practices that give rise to living hope.

Discussion

1. Which of the six reasons for hope grabbed your attention the most? What is it about this particular aspect of hope that caught your attention and stimulated your imagination?

2. Which reason for hope do you encounter most frequently in your church and community? Why do you think this aspect of hope predominates?

23. See Brueggemann, *A Gospel of Hope*.
24. Quoted from Fox, "Laudato Si."

3. What are the weaknesses in your church and community with regard to the reasons for hope? How might you live it out or bear witness to it more fully together?

4. If you were actually asked by someone to provide a reason for the hope that is in you, how would you respond? If the reason you give is your "strong suit," what is your "weak suit," and why does it not surface as much?

FOUR

THE PRACTICE OF HOPE

Hope, like love and faith, is an active verb. It implies engagement, not passivity. You don't simply sit and wait for hope to happen. If you do, it is likely to elude you. God invites you to live it out, to put it into practice. The beauty of hope emerges—blossoms might be a better word—whenever you participate in God's vision and mission. You discover the hope that lies within you when you take action, even if that means quite simply welcoming shalom into your heart and life. Hope begins in the act of opening your heart to the presence of the God of hope and peace.

The Hebrew word for hope—*yakhal*—means to wait or to trust. This is why it is so closely related to that other theological virtue, faith. Trust in Jesus and his way situates you in the space in which hope dwells. Participation in Christ ignites hope. It cannot do otherwise. Hope implies confidence. It expects wonderful and beautiful things. Hope orients your life to the future. But in a paradoxical kind of way, through hope the past meets the future in the present. Hope pulls things together and propels you forward. Hope has this existential quality. It exudes urgency. It lifts, illuminates, fills, liberates, sustains, inspires, empowers, connects. Hope, in other words, begs to be practiced. So here are five different practices in which God can work through the Spirit to inspire, encourage, and excite you to a life of living hope.

Lectio Divina on Hope

One of the best ways to practice hope is simply to pray, to immerse yourself in God's word, and then to put your spiritual learning into action. Prayer lifts the soul into the presence of God and elevates the spirit. God's word orients your life to the way of Jesus, which is the way of hope. One of the most popular forms of praying the word today is known as *lectio divina*. It involves all three dimensions of most practices alluded to above: engaging, reflecting, and acting. The term literally means "divine reading." The primary purpose of this ancient spiritual practice has always been to cultivate deep attentiveness to the God who speaks to us through the word. It fosters a receptive, imaginative, and loving spirit. It also facilitates your movement into concrete actions that both reflect and inspire hope. Classically, this discipline consists of four movements, *lectio* (reading), *oratio* (prayer), *meditatio* (meditation), and *contemplatio* (contemplation).

I recommend a simplified version of this meditative technique oriented around four simple words: proclaim, picture, ponder, practice. This adapted form of *lectio divina* moves intentionally from contemplation to action. It emphasizes the formation of a receptive spirit and the cultivation of hope. When used with stories from Scripture related to hope, this technique can open windows and doors to hope in your life. Here are simple instructions for each of the four movements in this form of prayer.

Before anything else, pray for the presence and guidance of the Holy Spirit.

Proclaim. Read the passage. We recommend that you actually read it out loud. It helps to actually hear the word "proclaimed."

Picture. Read the same text again, this time picturing yourself somewhere in the narrative. With which person do you identify? Where do you find yourself in the drama that is unfolding imaginatively before your eyes?

Ponder. After a third reading of the text, ponder what these words might mean for you today. What insight have you gained about yourself, God, your neighbor? What significance do you attach to your discoveries given your recent experiences, relationships, concerns?

Practice. Following a final reading of the passage, resolve to translate your experience in the meditation into action. What is God calling you to do with this today? What action is required? What does God require of you to live in and to be an ambassador of hope throughout the course of the day?

Close your meditation with a prayer for God's help and support as you seek to be faithful.

In order to enhance the connections of this practice to the biblical vision of hope, we invite you to meditate specifically on the following biblical passages. There are seven, so you may want to set apart one week and use these for your quiet time with God, one per day. Or you can stretch these out over a longer period of time if you wish. Listen for God's word of hope to you as you pray.

- Luke 7:11–17 (Jesus raises the widow's Son at Nain)
- Luke 8:49–55 (Jesus raises Jairus's daughter)
- Luke 13:10–17 (Jesus heals a crippled woman)
- Jeremiah 29:11–14 (a future with hope)
- Psalm 43:3–5 (hope in God)
- Romans 8:22–25 (awaiting hope with patience)
- Romans 15:13 (abounding in hope)

Martin Luther's Four-Stranded Garland

Luther developed a very similar prayer technique related to his sixteenth-century rediscovery of the Bible. When his barber and friend, Peter Beskendorf, asked him how to pray, he responded with a letter that he later published as a little tract entitled *A Simple Way to Pray*. Like *lectio divina*, this process consists of four movements or threads that Luther wove together to produce what he called a "four-stranded garland."

First, he recommended that you reflect upon a text with an open heart, looking for the specific instruction the Lord may have for you.

Second, give thanks to God with a grateful heart for all the possibilities laid out before you in the subject of your reflection.

Third, ask the Holy Spirit to reveal whatever sins you may need to confess relative to the topic.

Fourth, pray about how the Lord wants you to live out your discoveries in your daily life.

This simple pattern of reflection and prayer provides another way to practice hope in a more structured way. Luther actually suggested using this model of prayer in reflection on the Ten Commandments, and used the first commandment to illustrate the practice.

> I think of each commandment as, first, instruction, which is really what it is intended to be, and consider what the Lord God demands of me so earnestly. Second, I turn it into a thanksgiving; third, a confession; and fourth, a prayer. I do so in thoughts or words such as these:
>
> [*Instruction*] Here I earnestly consider that God expects and teaches me to trust him sincerely in all things and that it is his most earnest purpose to be my God. I must think of him in this way at the risk of losing eternal salvation. My heart must not build upon anything else or trust in any other thing, be it wealth, prestige, wisdom, might, piety, or anything else.
>
> [*Thanksgiving*] Second, I give thanks for his infinite compassion by which he has come to me in such a fatherly way and, unasked, unbidden, and unmerited, has offered to be my God, to care for me, and to be my comfort, guardian, help, and strength in every time of need. We poor mortals have sought so many gods and would have to seek them still if he did not enable us to hear him openly tell us in our own language that he intends to be our God. How could we ever—in all eternity—thank him enough!
>
> [*Confession*] Third, I confess and acknowledge my great sin and ingratitude for having so shamefully despised such sublime teachings and such a precious gift throughout my whole life, and for having fearfully provoked his wrath by countless acts of idolatry. I repent of these and ask for his grace.

[*Prayer*] Fourth, I pray and say: "O my God and Lord, help me by thy grace to learn and understand thy commandments more fully every day and to live by them in sincere confidence. Preserve my heart so that I shall never again become forgetful and ungrateful, that I may never seek after other gods or other consolation on earth or in any creature, but cling truly and solely to thee, my only God. Amen, dear Lord God and Father. Amen."[1]

In simply reading through these paragraphs, you have prayed the first commandment with Luther. Now set apart some time to pray each of the remaining nine in this same fashion, using these four movements. Luther most certainly viewed this model for prayer not only as an aid to the spiritual life, but as a way to inspire hope as you root yourself more firmly in God's way. He has gifted you with a helpful structure for your reflection, not a rigid formula to follow. Open your heart to the presence of the Holy Spirit as you engage in this practice of hope and follow the Spirit's lead.

If you would like to place this practice in a larger context, we highly recommend that you first read a chapter entitled "How Can We Learn to Live the Language of Focal Concerns?" in Marva Dawn's book *Unfettered Hope*. At the outset of that chapter, she explains,

> Now, in this chapter, we can turn to particular practices of Christianity by which we are lifted into hope and by which our character can be more deeply formed for the sake of developing culture positively and keeping the ravages and bondages of our technological, commodified society in check. . . . To organize this discussion of Christian practices, I have chosen to follow the pattern of the Ten Commandments. These mandates, underscored

1. Luther, "A Simple Way to Pray," in *Devotional Writings*, 200–201.

in both biblical Testaments, keep us centered in our focal concerns for loving God and the neighbor.[2]

Pondering Hope through Hymns and Sacred Songs

Psalms, hymns, and other sacred songs can be used for meditation and prayer related to hope in addition to their normal use as sung texts in worship services. You can engage this practice both individually, in the context of small groups, and as part of a worshiping community.

Individual Meditation

No season of the Christian year focuses attention on hope more than Advent, that preparatory season leading to the celebration of Jesus' birth at Christmas. Charles Wesley composed a beautiful hymn for this season, "Come, Thou Long-Expected Jesus." Meditating on the opening stanza of this hymn provides an illustration of how to ponder hope using a text like this one.

> Come, thou long-expected Jesus,
> Born to set thy people free,
> From our fears and sins release us,
> Let us find our rest in thee:
> Israel's strength and consolation,
> Hope of all the earth thou art,
> Dear desire of every nation,
> Joy of every longing heart.

Simply turn your pondering of these words into a conversation with God.

2. Dawn, *Unfettered Hope*, 145–46.

God, you come to me in the present moment in ways that always surprise, challenge, and inspire me. These words remind me of how others through the centuries have awaited your coming with such great hope. Sometimes I yearn so much for you in my life that the expectation is almost too much for me. My own needs and concerns press in upon me. The demands of my life sometimes overwhelm me. I long for your presence in the midst of it all. I hope, sometimes it seems beyond hope, for an appearance, a sign, a word, a presence. The Israelites, your own people, lived in that kind of collective expectation, and Wesley attempted to capture their feelings—my feelings—in this familiar hymn. You come, O God, and bring liberation from fear and sin. You offer rest and peace. You come with a desire to reign in my heart forever and to raise me up through the power of the Spirit.

O Loving God, I celebrate your advent throughout this journey of hope. Come, and renew my heart and mind through the presence of the Spirit of Christ. Amen.

There are many other hymns and contemporary songs, of course, for you to ponder as well, some of which we encountered in chapter 2. Simply follow the same process with these hymns and songs. Read or sing them, stanza by stanza, pausing at the conclusion of each verse to reflect on hope and what it means in your life. Or listen to the entirety of the song and reflect upon the whole. Here are a few suggestions.

- "All My Hope" (Michael Crowder)
- "Anchor—I Have This Hope" (Hillsong)
- "Be Still My Soul" (Katharine von Schlegel)
- "Be Thou My Vision" (Trad. Irish)
- "Hope of the World" (Georgia Harkness)
- "Hymn of Promise" (Natalie Sleeth)

- "My Hope Is You" (Third Day)

- "Jesus Christ, My Living Hope" (Phil Wickham)

- "O God, Our Help in Ages Past" (Isaac Watts)

- "O Love That Will Not Let Me Go" (George Matheson)

Consider making this exercise a regular practice in your life of devotion.

A Corporate Act of Living Hope

The staff of Discipleship Ministries of The United Methodist Church developed the following liturgical expression of hope using a hymn of Edward Mote, "My Hope Is Built," as a template interlined with Scripture passages from the book of Revelation.[3] This act stands alone as a practice of hope or can be incorporated into a full service of worship.

> "My Hope Is Built," stanza one:
> *My hope is built on nothing less than Jesus' blood and*
> *   righteousness.*
> *I dare not trust the sweetest frame, but wholly lean on*
> *   Jesus' name.*
> *On Christ the solid rock I stand, all other ground is sink-*
> *   ing sand.*
>
> Revelation 21:1-2, 23-24 (NRSV):
> Leader: Then I saw a new heaven and a new earth; for
> the first heaven and the first earth had passed away,
> and the sea was no more.
> *People: And I saw the holy city, the new Jerusalem, com-*
> *   ing down out of heaven from God, prepared as a bride*
> *   adorned for her husband.*

3. See "A Congregational Act of Living Hope."

Leader: And the city has no need of sun or moon to shine on it, for the glory of God is its light, and its lamp is the Lamb.

People: The nations will walk by its light, and the kings of the earth will bring their glory into it.

"My Hope Is Built," stanza two:

When darkness veils his lovely face, I rest on his unchanging grace.

In every high and stormy gale, my anchor holds within the veil.

On Christ the solid rock I stand, all other ground is sinking sand.

Revelation 21:3–4 (NRSV):

Leader: And I heard a loud voice from the throne saying, "See, the home of God is with mortals. God will dwell with them as their God; they will be God's peoples, and God will be with them;

People: God will wipe every tear from their eyes. Death will be no more, mourning and crying and pain will be no more, for the first things have passed away."

"My Hope Is Built," stanza three:

His oath, his covenant, his blood support me in the whelming flood.

When all around my soul gives way, he then is all my hope and stay.

On Christ the solid rock I stand, all other ground is sinking sand.

Revelation 21:5–6; 22:20 (NRSV):

Leader: And the one who was seated on the throne said, "See, I am making all things new. Write this, for these words are trustworthy and true."

People: Then he said to me, "I am the Alpha and the Omega, the beginning and the end."

Leader: The one who testifies to these things says, "Surely I am coming soon."

People: Amen. Come, Lord Jesus!

"My Hope Is Built," stanza four:
When he shall come with trumpet sound, O may I then in
*   him be found!*
Dressed in his righteousness alone, faultless to stand
*   before the throne!*
On Christ the solid rock I stand, all other ground is sink-
*   ing sand.*

There is also a "Canticle of Hope" in The United Methodist Hymnal (734), based on Revelation as well, that can be used in this way.

Gathering Signs of Hope Exercise

One way to engage in the practice of hope is to share an experience of gathering signs of hope. The idea for this practice comes from the work of Ben Campbell Johnson.[4] The exercise provides an opportunity for you to incorporate signs of hope into an expanded life of prayer that relates directly to the ordinary events and decisions of your daily life. It includes both time for individual reflection and then, if you wish, for sharing with others in the context of a small group. Altogether, it consists of five movements.

You conduct the first three movements as individuals in the comfort of your own home in a way that is meaningful and helpful to you. You engage the optional, but highly recommended, final two movements together as a small group in a weekly meeting set at a convenient time for all involved. So you need to form a small group of close friends if you wish to take this practice to a deeper level. For the purposes of this exercise, the group should be no more than four people and may be as

---

4. Johnson, *Invitation to Pray*, 18–22 in particular.

small as two. Set aside an hour or hour and a half on the same day each week to meet for reflection and prayer.

Three Individualized Movements

Set aside time each day in the evening prior to retiring for the night to review the events of the day and your response to them. Alternatively, you can make a review of the previous day the following morning, if you prefer.

1. Gather the day. Identify two or three signs of hope that you witnessed or experienced. Simply list those things that come immediately to mind, that are right "on your heart."

2. Review the day. Reflect upon each of these signs, reviewing your response to them. What feelings did they elicit? What words did you speak? What actions did you take?

3. Give thanks for the day. Take time to thank God for these experiences of hope and for God's presence in the midst of it all. Write down a brief prayer thanks to God.

Two Small Group Movements

4. Share your sightings. From among the many "sightings of hope" you have written about and reflected upon during your individual time from the previous week (since you last met), write down one or two actions or events that particularly inspired you. Share these in your group. Pray together, giving thanks to God for these signs of hope and the way they are shaping your lives.

5. Seek the meaning. After you have had an opportunity to pray, reflect together on the larger significance of these events in your life. Each person identifies, writes down, and talks about just one event or sign of hope in this regard, either their own or someone else's. Ask yourselves the following questions in turn: What is God saying to me in this event? What am I being called to do? How is this connected to the rest of my life? After you have each had an opportunity to share, pray for one another that God through the power of the Holy Spirit will confirm the insight and enable you to grow more fully into the hope-filled image of Christ.

The Practice of Beauty

Nothing restores hope like spending time in nature. Beauty inspires hope. It lifts your spirit. Experiencing the sunshine, a gentle rain, the shade of a tree, a cool breeze, the song of the birds, the babbling of a brook or the rhythmic sound of the waves upon the beach, sunrise and sunset—God renews your hope through all these means. Creation heals.

Walking also heals. The evidence is actually quite overwhelming in terms of the benefits and restorative qualities of this simple exercise. Walking also has a longstanding connection with prayer. Trish Brown, in her survey of various *Paths to Prayer*, offers some really helpful examples of "Prayer Walks."[5] Walking gets you out into God's creation. God will meet you in your walk, walk alongside you, help you see the beauty, and deeply desire to restore your hope. Here is how the practice of beauty and hope through a prayer walk in nature works.[6]

First, decide where and when to walk. Most communities, even major urban centers, have parks and green spaces specifically designed to help you experience the beauty of nature.

Second, be intentional about activating your attentiveness. Most of the time, as we are zooming around, taking care of business and the chores of life, we drop our attentive focus. We don't see things or notice what's around us. We become focused

---

5. Brown, *Paths to Prayer*, 209–13.

6. Some of you may not be able to "get out into nature," either because of infirmity or circumstance. But beauty, creation, nature can come to you. Simply google "meditation on nature," "nature therapy," or even "relaxation," and you will be amazed how many ten-minute to three-hour video presentations you can enjoy. Whether you are out in the woods on a walk or taking a virtual walk through nature with the help of technology, God will show up and resurrect hope in your soul.

on the task and not the journey. A prayer walk provides the opportunity to reverse this process. Open your eyes. Tune up your ears. Touch things. Breathe deeply and enjoy the smells (particularly in the spring!).

Third, breathing is actually an important part of walking prayer. As Trish Brown observes: "When we breathe in thanksgiving, we unite our breath with an invocation to the Holy Spirit, willing God to awaken our own spirit. As you begin to walk, give God thanks for your breath and the ability to move your body. Moving further into your walk, unite the rhythm of your gait with the rhythm of your breath."[7]

Fourth, that act of thanksgiving is actually a critical part of rediscovering hope. Thanksgiving and hope are integrally connected.

Fifth, take notice of all the beauty that surrounds you. Take joy in the colors. Pause from time to time to inspect whatever has drawn your attention. Celebrate the myriad forms of life that are a part of this created world. Absorb all that surrounds you, remembering that all you see and feel and hear is of God. All you experience is worthy of prayer and thanksgiving. Smell the roses.

Finally, as Brown suggests, "As you near the end of your prayer walk, consciously release your own agenda and choose to accept the will of God. Only when you let go of your own plans and desires with every breath and consequently step out in faith, embracing God's peace and hope will you know the wealth of both giving and receiving."[8]

7. Brown, *Paths to Prayer*, 211.
8. Brown, *Paths to Prayer*, 212.

The Practice of Nonviolence

In a world bereft of hope, many find it through the practice of nonviolent resistance to evil. The voiceless are given hope when they hear others speaking up on their behalf. The marginalized find encouragement when people stand with them. People considered to be "others" by prejudiced people recover a sense of their sacred worth when they are treated as fellow siblings in the human family. But the oppressed and forgotten ones are not the only ones given renewed hope; so too are those who practice nonviolence, seeking to restore beloved community in those places where it is absent.

Hope revives when "the kingdoms of this world" are subverted by life in the kingdom of God. Hope is rekindled when injustice is replaced by justice. Hope grows in the soil where evil is overcome with good. Hope encircles the earth whenever we come together to say "No!" to egotism and ethnocentrism. Richard Rohr has recently captured the spirit and substance of this practiced vision:

> Faith, hope, and love are the very nature of God, and thus the nature of all Being.
> Such goodness cannot die.
> No one religion will ever encompass the depth of such faith.
> No ethnicity has a monopoly on such hope.
> No nationality can control or limit this flow of universal love.[9]

Even though we may have failed to recognize it at the time, we received our marching orders for this kind of living when we were baptized. We made vows to resist evil in whatever forms it presents itself. Baptism marks our entry into nonviolent

9. Rohr, "Jesus, Christ, and the Beloved Community," 1.

resistance, our means of making real what we mean when we pray, "Thy kingdom come, thy will be done on earth as it is in heaven." And surely, wherever we do God's will, hope thrives!

John Dear has become a leader for nonviolent resistance in our day. In his book *Living Peace*, he links the practice of nonviolence with the offering of hope.[10] He is bold to say that it is not until we are willing to put feet to our convictions that we become believable, and until we are believable we cannot be bearers of hope in the world. While applying this conviction to our day, John is only repeating the sentiment of St. Francis, who said essentially the same thing in his well-loved prayer:

> Lord, make me an instrument of your peace.
> Where there is hatred, let me sow love.
> Where there is injury, pardon.
> Where there is doubt, faith.
> Where there is despair, hope.
> Where there is darkness, light.
> Where there is sadness, joy.
> O Divine Master,
> grant that I may not so much seek to be consoled as to console,
> to be understood as to understand,
> to be loved as to love.
> For it is in giving that we receive,
> It is in pardoning that we are pardoned,
> and it is in dying that we are born to eternal life. Amen.

We bring our suggested practices to a close by commending your involvement in nonviolent living. There are groups in your denomination, your congregation, and in your community waiting for someone like you to join them. Discover them online. Contact them directly. Attend their meetings. Join their

---

10. Dear, *Living Peace*, 214–21 (chapter 25, "Hope Upon Hope").

journey. Become a hope giver, and in doing so, you will find it yourself: "Give, and it will be given you" (Luke 6:38).

We pray that you meet the God of hope in these practices. Open yourself to the presence of the Spirit. God will lift you up, renew your hope, and prepare you to be a beacon of hope to others.

> May the God of hope fill you with all joy and peace in
> believing,
> so that you may abound in hope by the power of the Holy
> Spirit. (Rom 15:13 NRSV)

A HOPE-FILLED FUTURE

T his is volume three of a trilogy that celebrates active faith, living hope, and holy love.[1] In his monumental *Summa Theologica*, the great medieval theologian Thomas Aquinas described faith, hope, and love as theological virtues because they all have God for their object. All three bring us into God's presence. But God also forms these virtues in our lives as we apprentice ourselves to Jesus under the power of the Spirit. Charles Wesley taught the early Methodist people to sing about "Faith's assurance, hope's increase, / All the confidence of love!"[2] While St. Paul clearly affirms that love is "the greatest of these," all three actually work together to restore the image of God and hope in our lives.

Our prayer is that this book has *increased* your hope. If you began reading this book as someone who had lost hope, we pray you have found it anew. Wesley often uses the phrase "prisoner of hope" to describe the faithful follower of Jesus.[3] We

---

1. If you have not read *Active Faith* and *Holy Love*, we hope you will include them in your reading program for spiritual enrichment and growth. Both books may be purchased directly from any major online bookstore.

2. Wesley, *Hymns and Sacred Poems* (1739), 112.

3. Wesley, *Hymns and Sacred Poems* (1740), 40.

pray that hope has captured you and will never let you go. But we are not only prisoners, we are partners. God rejoices when we accept that invitation to partner in the ministry of proclaiming and inspiring hope in everyone we encounter. "Partners of a glorious hope, / Lift your hearts and voices up."[4] Most certainly, we have the privilege to provide a reasoned account for the hope within us. But the hope to which we point is something more glorious, wonderful, and beautiful than anything we can imagine.

Hopelessness and despair, unfortunately, characterize life for so many of God's beloved children on this globe. So many seek frantically for just a glimmer of hope, anywhere. They long for a beacon of hope as they flounder in a sea of despair. There are no easy answers, either outside or inside the church. But we find it to be particularly painful when the church falls prey to the polarization and fear that seem to dominate our lives today. We believe that God has given us a higher calling. So we long, too, for a church that is faithful to the way of Jesus—a church that exudes grace and imitates the inclusiveness and unconditional love of Jesus. This authentic face of the Christian faith plants seeds of living hope everywhere.

In the midst of life's struggles, one thing remains absolutely clear. Jesus Christ will always be the substance of our hope, the ground of authentic Christian discipleship, and the foundation of the church. Our hope, therefore, cannot be dashed by division or trampled by tribulation. Our hope is in Christ, and God promises us today, just as God promised his despairing children in exile:

4. Wesley, *Hymns and Sacred Poems* (1740), 184.

A Hope-Filled Future

> I know the plans I have in mind for you,
> declares the Lord;
> they are plans for peace, not disaster,
> to give you a future filled with hope. (Jer 29:11)

We praise God for this living hope.

HOPE IN THE MIDST OF A PANDEMIC

None of us could ever have predicted that, as this book was in production, we would experience a global pandemic. It only seemed appropriate to add this word in light of this unprecedented development because it touches on concerns related to hope so deeply.

Nothing exacerbates hopelessness like isolation. God made us for each other. Relationship defines God and all of us, as we are created in God's image. Many of the stories of hope you have read in this book derive from connections that men, women, and children have made with one another. Relationships generate and feed hope. In Scripture and in our narratives about life, one of the primary sources of hope is our connectedness. Our relationships with people catalyze hope.

So what can you do in a situation of imposed orders to "shelter at home" or "stay safe in isolation"? How do you find hope in the midst of this COVID-19 pandemic? How do you find strength and hope when you are separated from your community of faith in this time of "physical distancing"? Several reminders are extremely important.

1. *You are not alone or isolated.* Despite the fact that you may be physically distant, you can still feel close to others. You already know this. In some ways, this crisis might be teaching us more than ever before about the interconnectedness of life. It can even lead you to celebrate those connections in ways you have taken for granted. Just to give one example, we have been so inspired by the numerous "virtual choirs" that have formed online during these days. We have learned that, even though separated by thousands of miles, we can lift up our voices together in song. Those songs generate hope.

2. *Reach out to one another in love.* Take this unprecedented moment to connect with someone you have not talked with in some time. Reconnect with family members who are distant, but as close as a smart phone or a computer screen. You may be part of a family with children. In "normal" circumstances your children are far from you more than they are near during the course of the day. The same may be true of your spouse. Use this time to rediscover the joy of family (and the need to cultivate patience). When the walls begin to close you in, brainstorm ways to play and talk, to cook and eat together. If you are single, use an application that provides the opportunity for you to talk with a group online. Set a date and time to "be" with others. The simple act of reaching out fosters hope.

3. *Limit your media intake.* In the previous point, we celebrated the miracles of a technological world. Technology can be an amazing tool of connection. But media can also bring you down quickly. You could easily watch

twenty-four-hour news channels and immerse yourself in the angst of the moment. Don't! Bombarding your heart, mind, and spirit with this "cacophony of sound" saps hope from you. St. Paul's advice to the Philippians addresses this issue rather directly: "If anything is excellent and if anything is admirable, focus your thoughts on these things: all that is true, all that is holy, all that is just, all that is pure, all that is lovely, and all that is worthy of praise" (4:8). Beauty and loveliness nurture hope.

4. *Remind yourself that we will get through this.* Pandemics are marathons, not sprints. We have heard health professionals say this often. That means you must pace yourself. Plan your time. Focus on what you can control. When Paul was a boy he had rheumatic fever. He ended up in the hospital for what, to him, seemed like an eternity. But he was released, actually on an Easter afternoon. Laying in the back seat of the car on his ride home, he was able to see the forsythia in full blossom all along the route. Just before the pandemic hit, Steve and his wife, Jeannie, made a trip to Sevilla, Spain, to celebrate their fiftieth wedding anniversary. Little did they know that they would find themselves confined there for weeks. Nevertheless, they made new friends and joined in the applause with their neighbors on their balcony every evening in support of the frontline heroes who carry on for the sake of others. This too shall pass. We will get through this. All day long God is at work for good in this. Open your eyes to see God at work, through the lives of others who offer random acts of

kindness, in the beauty of nature that surrounds us all, and in the promise of a future filled with hope.

While this addendum speaks directly to the situation in which we are currently living, we may very well face similar circumstances in the future for which we will be better prepared. You can approach these days, therefore, as a school of hope. Ask God to attune your heart to the new dimensions of hope you are experiencing every day. At the end of each day ask yourself, "How did I experience hope today? What was it that created an uplifting spirit of hope?" Express your thanks to God for the hope brought to you by others. Thank the "hope-bearers" and seek to be a hope-bearer yourself. That, in and of itself, might change a life.

A WORD TO THOSE IN DESPAIR

You may be in despair today. We are truly sorry about your situation and the circumstances that have dampened your hope and left you in a place of darkness. We have been there, and return there ourselves from time to time. Everyone has felt hopeless; everyone needs hope. We do not believe God intends you to remain in this darkness—in this despair—without hope. We genuinely pray that this book has brought some comfort, some solace, and planted a seed of hope in your life.

Despair comes, of course, in all shapes and sizes. It can be psychological, emotional, or relational in nature. Despair leads to depression and depression leads to despair. Neither of us is a professional counselor or psychologist; we are pastors and teachers in the church. But if you sense that the darkness overwhelming you comes from spaces of personal brokenness, woundedness, or harm, we encourage you to seek professional as well as spiritual help. God uses both to help you recover a sense of well-being and a vision of a future filled with hope.

The world in which we live can easily dash our hopes; is it not a dream-killer at times? The current polarization and animosity, tension and division, drain the hope out of us. God does not intend the world to be like this, and in the face of these forces God works for good all day long. So God is out there—and in you—a light, a force, a power for hope. We just need to be on the lookout every day for God's presence and then partner with God in this grand project of hope-restoration.

Unfortunately, despair invades the church as well, and these same hope-depleting forces at work in the world affect the community of faith. And we want to speak a particular word into the life of the church today—even into the life of our own beloved United Methodist Church. In these days of tension, anxiety, and dis-ease, we have a word of hope regardless of what happens. Whether the church experiences division or finds a way to express its unity in Christ in more tangible ways, God still offers a vision of hope in Christ. God ties that hope, we believe, directly to our primary mission in the world, namely, making disciples of Jesus Christ for the transformation of the world. So, that common mission includes a partnership with God—as St. Francis reminds us—that turns *injury into pardon, error into truth, doubt into faith, despair into hope, darkness into light, and sadness into joy. This is precisely why St. Paul proclaims that* "hope does not disappoint us, because God's love has been poured into our hearts through the Holy Spirit that has been given to us" (Rom 5:5 NRSV). And then he prays, "May the God of hope fill you with all joy and peace in believing, so that you may abound in hope by the power of the Holy Spirit" (Rom 15:13 NRSV).

If you find yourself despairing because of circumstances in the world or in the church, take heart. God's love, joy, and peace—God's hope—will triumph in the end. God will restore all creation to the harmonious community of love intended from the very beginning. In response to God's vision and as participants in God's mission, therefore, we advocate an inclusive church in which every person feels welcome, appreciated, and loved. We want you to remember each and every day that you are a beloved child of God. You can have confidence because Christ is our hope, not only for the church but for the world. You can sing these words of Georgia Harkness with eager anticipation and great expectation. Join in this song—fill the world with this chorus of living hope:

> Hope of the world, thou Christ of great compassion,
> Speak to our fearful hearts by conflict rent.
> Save us, thy people, from consuming passion,
> Who by our own false hopes and aims are spent.
>
> Hope of the world, God's gift from highest heaven,
> Bringing to hungry souls the bread of life,
> Still let thy spirit unto us be given,
> To heal earth's wounds and end our bitter strife.
>
> Hope of the world, afoot on dusty highways,
> Showing to wandering souls the path of light,
> Walk thou beside us lest the tempting byways
> Lure us away from thee to endless night.
>
> Hope of the world, who by thy cross didst save us
> From death and dark despair, from sin and guilt,
> We render back the love thy mercy gave us;
> Take thou our lives, and use them as thou wilt.
>
> Hope of the world, O Christ o'er death victorious,
> Who by this sign didst conquer grief and pain,
> We would be faithful to thy gospel glorious;
> Thou art our Lord! Thou dost forever reign.[5]

5. Words: Georgia Harkness © 1954, Ren. 1982 The Hymn Society (Admin. Hope Publishing Company, Carol Stream, IL 60188). All rights reserved. Used by permission.

APPENDIX B
A WORD TO THOSE WHO HAVE HOPE

I f you are filled with hope today, that means you have an amazing gift to share with the world. You can be absolutely certain that you have neighbors, colleagues at work, family members in your own home, and friends young and old for whom hope is in short supply today. Think of yourself as a beacon of hope. Embrace God's call upon you to be a hope-bearer. Hope, like love, as we've seen, grows as you give it away. So share it lavishly with others. It doesn't take a huge amount of effort to do this. You can communicate your own hope through a smile, a kind word, an act of thoughtfulness. Consider the great joy of helping restore hope in someone else's life. You can be a hope-instiller—hope-preserver—and that gift of hope might even preserve life today.

Light and hope are much alike. Light dispels darkness and hope dispels despair. Since you have been in darkness yourself, even in the depths of despair perhaps, you know how essential hope can be. Some people are very good at covering up or disguising the darkness and despair in which they live daily. But, for the most part, it is not difficult to identify people who live in this land of shadows. So, keep your eyes open and your spiritual sense awake. If you have hope, even the smallest glimmer of light, all you have to do is be authentic. That hope will radiate from you of its own accord. Hope and love always work in this way when you become transparent to the presence of God within. So just be your hope-filled self, and cast the seeds of living hope about wherever you go.

We have a particular concern about excluded folks. For them, despair is all too frequently their constant companion. Every single human being wants to feel that he, she, they belong. We have an opportunity either to provide hospitality for those who find themselves on the outside or to accentuate their feelings of desperation because of our hostility. When we—and even more particularly the church—create barriers or draw lines that keep people out, we inflict untold harm and steal the gift of hope that God offers freely to all people. We invite you into actions, therefore, that subvert exclusivity and thereby open pathways to the rediscovery of hope. Simple acts of inclusion, offered to those who have never felt they were part of the inner circle—or any circle for that matter—heal, restore, renew, and uplift. They are signs of hope, they instill hope, and they proclaim God's vision of living hope.

One of Mother Teresa's favorite prayers has come to be known as the "Fragrance Prayer." It is actually her adaptation of a prayer poem entitled "Radiating Christ," written originally by Cardinal John Henry Newman. She prayed this prayer every day after Eucharist with her Sisters of Charity, simply exchanging the singular of Newman's poem for a plural form of the words so it could be used in community. We offer this prayer

to you as a gift. Pray it often. It is the prayer of our own hearts.
Let's pray this prayer together and often so that we might become God's instruments of hope and love in the world.

> Dear Jesus, help us to spread your fragrance everywhere we go.
> Flood our souls with your spirit and life.
> Penetrate and possess our whole being so utterly,
> that our lives may only be a radiance of yours.
>
> Shine through us, and be so in us,
> that every person we should come in contact with
> may feel your presence in our soul.
> Let them look up and see no longer us, but only Jesus.
>
> Stay with us, and then we shall begin to shine as you shine;
> so to shine as to be a light to others;
> the light, Jesus, will be all from you.
> None of it will be ours.
> It will be you shining on others through us.
>
> Let us thus praise you in the way you love best,
> by shining on those around us.
> Let us preach you without preaching:
> not by words, but by our example,
> by the catching force,
> the sympathetic influence of what we do,
> the evident fullness of the love our hearts bear for you.
> Amen.[6]

6. See "Fragrance Prayer (Cardinal Newman/Mother Teresa)."

FOR FURTHER READING

This simple list of resources reflects some of the more important books that have shaped our theology and practice of living hope. We reference most of them in the narrative of each chapter and have organized them around those primary themes. Your exploration of these books can be an extension of your practice of living hope.

The Witness to Hope

Walter Brueggemann, *A Gospel of Hope*

Walter Brueggemann, *Interrupting Silence: God's Command to Speak Out*

Walter Brueggemann, *Reality, Grief, Hope: Three Urgent Prophetic Tasks*

John Dear, *The Beatitudes of Peace: Meditations on the Beatitudes, Peacemaking & the Spiritual Life*

E. Stanley Jones, *Abundant Living*

Thomas Merton, *No Man Is an Island*

Pope Francis, *Open Mind, Faithful Heart: Reflections on Following Jesus*

The Legacy about Hope

Paul W. Chilcote, *The Wesleyan Tradition: A Paradigm for Renewal*

Jürgen Moltmann, *Ethics of Hope*

Jürgen Moltmann, *The Spirit of Hope: Theology for a World in Peril*

Jürgen Moltmann, *Theology of Hope*

Barack Obama, *The Audacity of Hope: Thoughts on Reclaiming the American Dream*

Natalie Sleeth, *Adventures for the Soul*

Elie Wiesel, *Night Trilogy*

The Reason for Hope

Walter Brueggemann, *From Judgment to Hope: A Study on the Prophets*

Walter Brueggemann, *Tenacious Solidarity: Biblical Provocations on Race, Religion, Climate, and the Economy*

Frederick Buechner, *Wishful Thinking: A Seeker's ABC*

E. Stanley Jones, *The Divine Yes*

Parker Palmer, *The Company of Strangers: Christians and the Renewal of America's Public Life*

Ronald Rolheiser, *Wrestling with God: Finding Hope and Meaning in Our Daily Struggles to Be Human*

For Further Reading

David Steindl-Rast, *Gratefulness, the Heart of Prayer: An Approach to Life in Fullness*

The Practice of Hope

Dorothy Bass, *Practicing Our Faith: A Way of Life for a Searching People*

Dorothy Bass, *Receiving the Day: Christian Practices for Opening the Gift of Time*

Patricia Brown, *Paths to Prayer: Finding Your Own Way to the Presence of God*

Marva Dawn, *Unfettered Hope: A Call to Faithful Living in an Affluent Society*

John Dear, *Living Peace: A Spirituality of Contemplation and Action*

Ben Campbell Johnson, *Invitation to Pray*

Miroslav Volf and Dorothy Bass, *Practicing Theology: Beliefs and Practices in Christian Life*

BIBLIOGRAPHY

Augustine, Saint. *Sermons*. Vol. 5 of *The Works of Saint Augustine: A Translation for the 21st Century; Part III*, edited by John E. Rotelle and translated by Edmund Hill, 222–37. Hyde Park, NY: New City, 1992.

Babcock, Maltbie D. "This Is My Father's World." In *The United Methodist Hymnal*. Nashville: United Methodist Publishing House, 1989.

Barclay, William. *The Letters to the Corinthians*. Daily Study Bible. Philadelphia: Westminster, 1954.

———. *New Testament Words*. London: SCM, 1964.

Bowie, Fiona. *Beguine Spirituality*. New York: Crossroad, 1990.

Brown, Patricia D. *Paths to Prayer: Finding Your Own Way to the Presence of God*. San Francisco: Jossey-Bass, 2003.

Brown, Raymond. *The Message of Numbers: Journey to the Promised Land*. Downers Grove: InterVarsity, 2002,

Brueggemann, Walter. *From Judgment to Hope: A Study on the Prophets*. Louisville: Westminster John Knox, 2019.

———. *God, Neighbor, Empire: The Excess of Divine Fidelity and the Command of Common Good*. Waco: Baylor University Press, 2016.

———. *A Gospel of Hope*. Louisville: Westminster John Knox, 2018.

———. *Interrupting Silence: God's Command to Speak Out*. Louisville: Westminster John Knox, 2018.

———. *Journey to the Common Good*. Louisville: Westminster John Knox, 2010.

———. *Tenacious Solidarity: Biblical Provocations on Race, Religion, Climate, and the Economy*. Minneapolis: Fortress, 2018.

———. *Theology of the Old Testament*. Minneapolis: Augsburg Fortress, 2009.

Buechner, Frederick. *Wishful Thinking: A Seeker's ABC*. New York: Harper & Row, 1973.

Butler-Bass, Diana. *Grateful*. New York: HarperOne, 2018.

Catechism of the Catholic Church. New York: Doubleday, 1994.

Chilcote, Paul W. *Active Faith: Resisting 4 Dangerous Ideologies with the Wesleyan Way*. Nashville: Abingdon, 2019.

———, ed. *Early Methodist Spirituality: Selected Women's Writings*. Nashville: Kingswood, 2007.

Bibliography

————. "Eucharist and Formation." In *A Wesleyan Theology of the Eucharist: The Presence of God for Christian Life and Ministry*, edited by Jason E. Vickers, 183–201. Nashville: General Board of Higher Education and Ministry, 2016.

————, ed. *Her Own Story: Autobiographical Portraits of Early Methodist Women*. Nashville: Kingswood, 2001.

————, ed. *The Wesleyan Tradition: A Paradigm for Renewal*. Nashville: Abingdon, 2002.

"A Congregational Act of Living Hope." Discipleship Ministries, The United Methodist Church, Apr 16, 2013. https://www.umcdiscipleship.org/resources/a-congregational-act-of-living-hope.

Dawn, Marva J. *Unfettered Hope: A Call to Faithful Living in an Affluent Society*. Louisville: Westminster John Knox Press, 2003.

Dear, John. *The Beatitudes of Peace: Meditations on the Beatitudes, Peacemaking & the Spiritual Life*. New London, CT: Twenty-Third, 2016.

————. *Living Peace: A Spirituality of Contemplation and Action*. New York: Image, 2001.

Fox, Matthew. "Laudato Si' and the Via Transformativa, continued." *Daily Meditations*, Nov 13, 2019. https://dailymeditationswithmatthewfox.org/2019/11/13/laudato-si-and-the-via-transformativa-continued/.

"Fragrance Prayer (Cardinal Newman/Mother Teresa)." Global Christian Worship, Sep 5, 2016. https://globalworship.tumblr.com/post/150014175520/fragrance-prayer-cardinal-newmanmother-teresa.

Francis, Pope. *Open Mind, Faithful Heart: Reflections on Following Jesus*. New York: Crossroad, 2013.

————. "Papal Audience of 17 May 2017." http://w2.vatican.va/content/francesco/en/audiences/2017/documents/papa-francesco_20170517_udienza-generale.html.

Gablik, Suzi. *The Re-enchantment of Art*. New York: Thames and Hudson, 1991.

Garvey, Michael, ed. *Dorothy Day*. Modern Spirituality Series. Springfield, IL: Templegate, 1996.

Harper, Steve. *Holy Love: A Biblical Theology of Human Sexuality*. Nashville: Abingdon, 2019.

Havel, Vaclav. "An Orientation of the Heart." In *The Impossible Will Take a Little While: A Citizen's Guide to Hope in a Time of Fear*, edited by Paul Rogat Loeb, 82–90. New York: Basic, 2004.

Hawn, Michael. "History of Hymns: 'O Love That Wilt Not Let Me Go.'" Discipleship Ministries, The United Methodist Church, Jun 20, 2013. https://www.umcdiscipleship.org/resources/history-of-hymns-o-love-that-wilt-not-let-me-go.

Herzberger, Magda. *Survival*. Austin: 1st World Library, 2005.

Job, Rueben. *Three Simple Rules*. Nashville: Abingdon, 2007.

Johnson, Ben Campbell. *Invitation to Pray*. Decatur, GA: CTS, 1992.

Johnson, James Weldon. *God's Trombones: Seven Negro Sermons in Verse*. New York: Viking, 1927.

Bibliography

Jones, E. Stanley. *Abundant Living*. Nashville: Abingdon, 1990.

——. *The Christ of Every Road*. Nashville: Abingdon, 1930.

——. *The Christ of the Mount*. Nashville: Abingdon, 1958.

——. *The Divine Yes*. Nashville: Abingdon, 1975.

——. *Growing Spiritually*. Nashville: Abingdon, 1978.

——. *In Christ*. Nashville: Abingdon, 1961.

——. *The Unshakable Kingdom and the Unchanging Person*. Nashville: Abingdon, 1972.

King, Martin Luther, Jr. *Strength to Love*. New York: Harper & Row, 1963.

Lawson, James. "Notes from an Architect of Non-violence—The Forces of Violence Today." *Religica* (podcast), Nov 4, 2019. https://religica.org/religica-podcast/.

Luther, Martin. *Devotional Writings II*. Edited by Gustav K. Wiencke. Vol. 43 of *Luther's Works*. Philadelphia: Fortress, 1968.

Marty, Martin. "Could a Revived 'Theology of Hope' Restore Faith in Hopeless Times?" *Sightings*, Nov 4, 2019. https://um-insight.net/perspectives/could-a-revived-theology-of-hope-restore-faith-in-hopeless-t/.

Merton, Thomas. *No Man Is an Island*. New York: Harcourt, Brace, & Jovanovich, 1955.

Mounce, William. *Complete Expository Dictionary of Old & New Testament Words*. Grand Rapids: Zondervan, 2006.

Nouwen, Henri. "The Promise of Hope." *Now & Then* (podcast). Henri Nouwen Society, Sept 23, 2017. https://henrinouwen.org/now-then-henri-nouwen/.

Obama, Barack. *The Audacity of Hope: Thoughts on Reclaiming the American Dream*. New York: Vintage, 2008.

"Orphaned Children Reunite in the Name of Peace for Kenya." ZOE Empowers. https://zoeempowers.org/orphaned-children-unite-name-peace-kenya/.

Palmer, Parker. *The Company of Strangers: Christians and the Renewal of America's Public Life*. New York: Crossroad, 1981.

——. "Hope Is the Place Where Joy Meets the Struggle." *On Being*, Sept 19, 2017. https://onbeing.org/blog/parker-palmer-hope-is-the-place-where-joy-meets-the-struggle/.

Rohr, Richard. "Jesus, Christ, and the Beloved Community." *The Mendicant: A Publication of the Center for Action and Contemplation* 9 (2019) 1, 4.

Sleeth, Natalie. *Adventures for the Soul: 35 Inspirational Hymns and the Stories behind Them*. Carol Stream, IL: Hope Publishing, 1987.

Steindl-Rast, David. *Gratefulness, the Heart of Prayer: An Approach to Life in Fullness*. New York: Paulist, 1984.

Valente, Gianni, ed. *Without Him We Can Do Nothing: A Conversation about Being Missionaries in Today's World*. Rome: Fides, 2019.

Wesley, John. *The Methodist Societies: History, Nature, and Design*. Edited by Rupert E. Davies. Vol. 9 of *The Works of John Wesley*, 70–73. Nashville: Abingdon, 1989.

Bibliography

———. *Sermons IV (115–151)*. Edited by Albert C. Outler. Vol. 4 of *The Works of John Wesley*, 120–30. Nashville: Abingdon, 1987.

Wesley, John, and Charles Wesley. *Hymns and Sacred Poems*. London: Strahan, 1739.

———. *Hymns and Sacred Poems*. London: Strahan, 1740.

———. *Hymns on the Lord's Supper*. Bristol: Farley, 1745.